Chista

MW00997238

SOLDIER, STATESMAN, PEACEMAKER

SOLDIER, STATESMAN, PEACEMAKER

Leadership Lessons
from George C. Marshall

JACK ULDRICH

AMACOM AMERICAN MANAGEMENT ASSOCIATION

NEW YORK ★ ATLANTA ★ BRUSSELS ★ CHICAGO ★ MEXICO CITY
SAN FRANCISCO ★ SHANGHAI ★ TOKYO ★ TORONTO ★ WASHINGTON, D.C.

This publication is designed to provide accurate and authoritative
information in regard to the subject matter covered. It is sold with the
understanding that the publisher is not engaged in rendering legal,
accounting, or other professional service. If legal advice or other expert
assistance is required, the services of a competent professional person
should be sought.

Library of Congress Cataloging-in-Publication Data

Uldrich, Jack, 1964–
    Soldier, statesman, peacemaker : leadership lessons from George C.
Marshall / Jack Uldrich.—1st ed.
        p.   cm.
    Includes bibliographical references and index.
    ISBN-10: 0-8144-0857-5
    ISBN-13: 978-0-8144-0857-5
    1. Marshall, George C. (George Catlett), 1880–1959.   2. Leadership.
3. Generals—United States.   4. Statesmen—United States.   I. Title:
Leadership lessons from George C. Marshall.   II. Title.
HD57.7.U453   2005
658.4'092—dc22

                                                    2004030411

Printing number

10 9 8 7 6 5 4 3

Contents

Foreword

I've been asked on many occasions to name the people I admire most. Always, General George Catlett Marshall has been first on my list. Often—especially with younger audiences—it is clear that many do not recognize the name of arguably the greatest American of the 20th Century.

As a consequence, when Jack Uldrich asked me to write the foreword for *Soldier, Statesman, Peacemaker: Leadership Lessons from George C. Marshall,* I was honored to do so. In this small way, I can pay homage to a person to whom every person living in freedom today owes an incalculable debt of gratitude.

General Marshall's contributions to the Allied victory in both World Wars, particularly the second, are without equal. In the same vein, his service afterwards as Secretary of State, Secretary of Defense, and head of the American Red Cross were also profoundly important to securing the peace earned at such a terrible price.

These great accomplishments have been chronicled by many authors over the years, but rarely has the focus been on the character, personality traits, and management skills which enabled General Marshall to accomplish so much with near universal acclaim and admiration. This is what Jack Uldrich ably does in this singular analysis of a truly unique man of any time or place.

In this regard, Marshall's leadership and managerial accomplishments are simply without peer given the unprecedented scale of his responsibilities in World War II. Even so, the legendary stories of the General's sense of duty, self discipline, probity, and rectitude stand in stark contrast to the historical portraits of many of his self promoted contemporaries better known to later generations. Among the great personalities of his time, however, George Marshall was venerated above all others.

As an executive, he repeatedly demonstrated the highest levels of competence and intelligence. Marshall was a master of detail, demanding outstanding performance by subordinates most of whom Marshall had personally selected and rapidly promoted based on his interwar observations of the officer corps. The General bestowed—and received in return—extreme loyalty. He expected results, and accepted nothing less.

Throughout his life, most importantly it was his strength of character that lead General Marshall to always do the right thing, at the right time, or to select others able to do so. As the chief architect of victory in World War II and the primary savior of a devastated Europe, Marshall's success rested squarely on his lifetime of integrity, commitment, industry, and self-effacing leadership style. So respected was he that politicians, foreign leaders, generals and admirals, and the public at large trusted his word alone as good enough to warrant the expenditure of billions of dollars. His abilities were held in such esteem that the grand strategies for global victory and European reconstruction were largely those developed by General Marshall and adopted by the Allied powers at his behest.

The lessons to be learned from Marshall's life are profound for anyone involved in a management or leadership position. While it is doubtful an individual will ever again have such enormous direct responsibilities, George Marshall's words and deeds provide an unmatched positive foundation for anyone who aspires to a life of accomplishment and honorable service to others.

Frederick W. Smith, Chairman,
President, and CEO, FedEx Corporation

Acknowledgments

I start by thanking my good friend Sean Kershaw, executive director of the Citizens League, for unwittingly reintroducing me to George C. Marshall when he invited me to speak to a group of German Marshall Fund fellows in the spring of 2003. While preparing for the meeting, I became reacquainted with the depth and breadth of Marshall's extraordinary career and was motivated to help rekindle the legacy of this exceptional leader. I also want to thank Adrienne Hickey, my editor at AMACOM, for her constant support and keen insights. The book is better as a result of her candor, patience, professionalism, and persistence.

The book also would not have been possible without the incredible dedication of numerous scholars, soldiers, and statesmen who have written about George Marshall over the years. I am particularly indebted to Marshall's official biographer, Forrest Pogue, whose wonderful four-volume, 1,900-page biography is truly Herculean in scope and stands as the single best work on Marshall's life. I am also grateful for the scholarly works of Ed Cray and Mark Stoler, as well as the professional staff at the Marshall Foundation Library in Lexington, Virginia—especially Dr. Larry Bland—who was most helpful with his comments, suggestions, and insights. All errors are my responsibility alone.

Lastly, I reserve my greatest thanks for my beautiful wife, Cindy, and our two children, Sean and Meghan, who have never failed to support me with their unconditional love.

PART I : A Leader for the Ages

THE UNKNOWN
FAMOUS AMERICAN

*In war he was as wise and understanding in counsel as he was resolute
in action. In peace he was the architect who planned the restoration of
[the] battered European economy . . . [h]e has always fought victoriously
against defeatism, discouragement, and disillusion. Succeeding generations must not be allowed to forget his achievements and his example.*
—Winston Churchill, letter to Colonel John C. Hagan, July 30, 1958

★ ★ ★ ★ ★

Ralph Waldo Emerson once said that "great men exist that there may be greater men." I have always felt there was a strong element of truth to this statement and, as such, I have also believed there is much to be learned from the great men and women of history. This book is about one of those men: General of the Army and Secretary of State George Catlett Marshall.

Based on what other great men have said of Marshall, there was perhaps no greater man in the twentieth century. Winston Churchill called him the "organizer of victory" and "the last great American." Dwight D. Eisenhower said of Marshall, "Our people have never been so indebted to any other soldier." And Harry Truman referred to him as the "great one of the age."

A cursory review of his extraordinary life reveals why these accolades still ring true more than a half century after his death:

* As chief of staff of the United States Army before and during World War II, Marshall transformed the army

from a weak and poorly armed force of 175,000 into the most powerful military service in the history of mankind—an 8 1/3 million person juggernaut with a logistics system stretching 60,000 miles and an arsenal of the era's most advanced weapons.

* During the same period, he became America's preeminent global strategist. In addition to balancing the needs of five different theaters of war—and managing the egos and personalities of such men as Franklin Roosevelt, Winston Churchill, Douglas MacArthur, and George Patton—Marshall attained an unprecedented level of interservice cooperation between the army and navy, achieved unity of command among the Allied forces, and convinced all parties to pursue the "Germany first" approach to the war—a concept considered by many military historians to be the single most important strategic concept of the war.

* As secretary of state in 1947, he introduced the European Recovery Program, henceforth known as the Marshall Plan, to restore the European continent torn apart by war and nearing financial and political collapse. Many credit him with almost single-handedly "winning the peace" and securing America's stature as the world's sole political, economic, and military superpower.

* At various other times in his career, he served as the president's emissary to China, president of the American Red Cross, and secretary of defense. *Time* magazine

twice named George Marshall its Man of the Year—in 1943, at the height of World War II, and again in 1947, at the height of the Cold War.

* In 1953, he capped his extraordinary career by becoming the first professional soldier to ever be awarded the Nobel Peace Prize.

Surprisingly, in spite of these many accomplishments and the accolades of his peers and contemporaries, George Marshall—whom Tom Brokaw has referred to as the "godfather of the greatest generation"—has faded into the collective recesses of the American mind. If his name is recalled, it is primarily because of his association with the Marshall Plan.

It is altogether fitting that he is remembered for this historic and influential act—but his contributions to America and the world, as the previous list testifies, were so much greater.

History's oversight is, however, not so much Marshall's loss as it is *ours*. For as Colin Powell once said, "We have so much still to learn from General Marshall—from his character, from his courage, his compassion and his commitment to our nation, and his commitment to all humankind." Among the greatest lessons we can learn from Marshall are his nine principles of leadership:

* Doing the Right Thing: The Principle of Integrity

* Mastering the Situation: The Principle of Action

* Serving the Greater Good: The Principle of Selflessness

* Speaking Your Mind: The Principle of Candor

* Laying the Groundwork: The Principle of Preparation

* Sharing Knowledge: The Principle of Learning and Teaching

* Choosing and Rewarding the Right People: The Principle of Fairness

* Focusing on the Big Picture: The Principle of Vision

* Supporting the Troops: The Principle of Caring

He has been called the unknown famous American, but George C. Marshall is precisely the type of leader we need today. In an era when too many of our public and private leaders are more interested in serving themselves than society; more interested in short-term profits than long-term investments; and more interested in power than empowering others, it is useful—indeed necessary—to stop, study, and reflect upon those who have gone before us and lived a great and principled life.

George Marshall always told his officers that the best way to direct men was by "making them see the way to go." Based on this premise and a belief that "great men exist that there may be greater men," there is no better way for today's leaders and tomorrow's future leaders to "see the way to go" than to study the life of the greatest American of the twentieth century—the unknown famous American, George Catlett Marshall.

GEORGE C. MARSHALL

The Indispensable Man

George C. Marshall was at year's end the closest thing to "the indis-pensable man".

—*Time* magazine, in naming George Marshall
Man of the Year for 1943

The more I see and talk to him, the more certain I am he's the great one of the age.

—Harry S. Truman

★ ★ ★ ★ ★

At 4:45 a.m. on the morning of September 1, 1939, the first of one and a half million Nazi soldiers stormed over the German border and invaded Poland. An ocean away in Washington D.C., a town preoccupied with keeping America out of the "European conflict," it was 10:45 p.m. and George C. Marshall—on the eve of his inauguration as the chief of staff of the United States Army—was asleep, unaware that a global conflagration that would consume the better part of the world's resources and all of his personal energy for the next six years had just erupted.

When he was sworn in as the U.S. Army's highest officer just hours later, Marshall became the head of an army that was smaller than Bulgaria's. He inherited only 175,000 troops, and rifles were in such short supply that some of his troops had to drill with wooden sticks.

Over the course of the next six years, Marshall would trans-form the United States military into the most powerful fighting force the world had ever known. It would come to number 8 1/3 million men and women, its logistics system would stretch 60,000 miles, and its arsenal would include 129,000 bombers, 4,000 ships, 2.5 million jeeps, 12 million rifles, and two atomic bombs—the most destructive weapons ever created.[1]

With the Allied victory in 1945, Marshall's work was only half complete. He had helped win the war but now, he understood, he had an obligation to finish the job by securing a lasting peace. The task was easier said than done. Europe lay in ruins and disillusionment; discontent and distrust were rampant.

And so it was on June 5, 1947—a day in which Marshall was awarded an honorary doctorate from Harvard University and called "a soldier and statesman whose ability and character brook only one comparison in the history of the nation" (the unstated comparison was to George Washington)—that he outlined what would become known worldwide as the Marshall Plan.

One historian has said it was the most important foreign policy success of the postwar period because it transformed the nations of Western Europe "from poverty cases into partners" and created the foundation upon which a lasting peace in Europe could finally be built.[2]

The two dates—September 1, 1939 and June 5, 1947—bookend the most tumultuous period in the twentieth century and George Marshall, first as army chief of staff and then as secretary of state, was at or near the helm of power through it all. A brief review of the leadership he demonstrated through this period demonstrates its continued relevance for today's leaders.

  ∗ George Marshall was a man of integrity and always demonstrated moral courage. If a matter came down to "doing something right" or "doing the right thing," he always chose the latter.

* He acted when action was required. Marshall understood that an imperfect act taken quickly was often far superior to a perfect act taken later.

* He was selfless. The characteristic was not born out of a lack of ambition—Marshall was very ambitious and achieved most of his ambitions—but he never placed his own personal interests ahead of his country.

* He was candid. Marshall never shied away from telling people—especially superiors—what they *needed* to hear, not what they *wanted* to hear.

* He was passionate about preparation. Marshall had seen the ravages of war, so he understood that a leader needed to prepare people for the "unpreparable"—often in the face of great indifference or outright opposition.

* He was a lifelong learner and a great teacher. Marshall realized that leadership required constant self-improvement. Moreover, he appreciated that a person who could impart knowledge to others was exponentially more valuable to an organization than a person without that skill.

* He believed in equality of opportunity and rewards for people of merit. Marshall fast-tracked talented people not only because it was fair, but because it was in the best interest of the organization that those people be placed in leadership positions—regardless of age, gender, or race.

* He continuously asked the question: "What needs to be done?" Marshall then prioritized issues and always placed the greatest emphasis on those actions that would most quickly and efficiently achieve his strategic goals.

* Lastly, he never forgot about his troops in the field. Marshall understood that "morale was primarily a function of command," and he saw to it that his people were provided for, recognized, rewarded, and appreciated.

The first part of Marshall's career—the thirty-four years he labored in obscurity and struggled under the army's seniority-laden promotion system before becoming a general officer—is equally instructive and will be given a good deal of coverage in this book because the same principles Marshall employed at the height of his power were also evident from the time he was a young second lieutenant.

As such, Marshall's life is just as relevant for today's college graduates and mid-level managers as it is for senior executives because it demonstrates that true leaders find a way to lead regardless of their position, stature, or age.

Therefore, before proceeding, a short refresher on the life of George Marshall is in order.

The Early Years

Marshall was born in Uniontown, Pennsylvania, on December 31, 1880. One biographer called his early childhood "unremarkable" and said he demonstrated no special skill or possessed no

unique characteristic that would have suggested future greatness. In fact, only later in life did Marshall offer any hint to his
ambition, remarking once that his father's "continuous harping
on the name of John Marshall [the famous Supreme Court justice—and a distant relative of George Marshall's] was a poor
kind of business" and he felt "[i]t was about time for somebody
to swim for the family again."

Marshall's choice of a career is similarly uninspired. He
chose to attend the Virginia Military Institute (VMI) for college because his older brother, Stuart—in a conversation that
Marshall happened to overhear—pleaded with his mother not
to let him attend his alma mater because he thought his
younger brother would "disgrace the family name." Marshall
later admitted the conversation "had quite a psychological
effect on my career" because he decided then and there that he
was going to "wipe [Stuart's] eye" by besting his brother's performance at VMI.

At VMI, Marshall continued his unexceptional academic
career but began to demonstrate an unusual talent for leadership. After his first year, he was selected first corporal, and by
his senior year, he had risen to first captain—VMI's highest-
ranking cadet.

LABORING IN OBSCURITY

The first fifteen years of Marshall's career were a study in
endurance, persistence, and patience. He labored in foreign and
distant outposts and was not promoted to the rank of captain
until 1916. Through it all, however, Marshall made the most of
every opportunity.

He was first assigned to a remote garrison in the Philippines where he gained valuable experience managing soldiers. The tour was followed by two years in the rugged and harsh terrain on the American frontier, where he surveyed and mapped the heart of the Texas badlands. In both jobs, his concern for the troops under his command—a trait he would consistently demonstrate throughout his career—was already evident.

Marshall received his first career break when he was selected to attend the Army Infantry and Cavalry School at Fort Leavenworth in 1906. The most junior officer in a distinguished group that included a number of other future generals, Marshall assiduously applied himself and "learned how to learn." His diligence was rewarded with a two-year extension, and he served as an instructor at the staff college. It was here that his skills as a teacher began to be honed.

During the summers, he was an instructor at National Guard camps, and following his schooling, Marshall went on to serve with the Massachusetts Voluntary Militia. It was the beginning of a life-long association with civilians. In 1913, Marshall was dispatched a second time to the Philippines and served as an aide to Major General Hunter Liggett. It was his first high-level staff position and he quickly demonstrated his aptitude and skill for the job.

THE WIZARD

In 1916, Marshall returned to the United States as Major General J. Franklin Bell's aide, and in early 1917, he and Bell were ordered to New York where Marshall helped with the effort to mobilize American troops for the First World War. It was his introduction to the practical aspects of preparing a nation for war.

In June 1917, Marshall departed for France with the First Division, where he served in a variety of different capacities in the war. His career took a sudden and unexpected turn when he came to the attention of General John J. Pershing, the head of the American Expeditionary Forces, because of a rather remarkable outburst of candor. (The story is covered in greater detail in Chapter 4).

While on Pershing's staff, Marshall received two quick wartime promotions and, in 1918, was called upon to plan and organize the largest American land offensive maneuver of World War I—the Meuse-Argonne offensive. The maneuver, for which Marshall received the nickname "the Wizard," caught the Germans completely by surprise and is credited with hastening the end of the war.

After the war, Marshall—whom Pershing later said was "the finest officer that the war produced"—was asked to serve as one of Pershing's top aides. It was a position he would hold for the next five years and served as a priceless indoctrination into the subtleties, nuances, and complexities of national and international politics.

In 1924, Marshall was sent to Asia for a third time—this time serving with the Fifteenth Infantry Regiment in Tientsin, China. During this period, Marshall learned Chinese and familiarized himself with many of the political problems that would continue to plague China for the remainder of the twentieth century.

In 1927, he was asked to serve as an instructor at the Army War College but, to help him recover from the sudden death of his wife, was reassigned to Fort Benning as head of instruction of the Army Infantry School. During his five years at Fort

Benning, Marshall revamped and modernized the school's curriculum. He also began noting those young officers whom he felt demonstrated initiative and flexibility and whose services might be called upon in the event of another war.

In 1930, Marshall remarried and two years later became the commanding officer at Fort Screven, Georgia. With the Depression worsening and the election of Franklin D. Roosevelt, he found that his command responsibilities were suddenly expanded when he was ordered to oversee work with the Civilian Conservation Corps (CCC). Unlike many army officers of the time—who considered the job of working with civilians to be beneath them—Marshall relished the opportunity. He continued in a similar position, albeit with greater responsibilities, the following year, when he was appointed commander at Fort Moultrie, South Carolina.

In 1933, Marshall was ordered to Chicago to serve as senior instructor to the Illinois National Guard. Fortified in his belief that civilians would comprise the bulwark of any wartime army, Marshall continued to hone his talent for working with civilians.

In 1936, after nearly three-and-a-half decades, his hard work finally paid off when he was promoted to brigadier general and awarded command of the Fifth Brigade of the Third Division at Fort Vancouver, Washington. For two years, Marshall savored the opportunity to again lead troops and work with the CCC.

The Beginning of Greatness

Two years later, in 1938, Marshall's career began to take off when he was recalled from his post in the Pacific Northwest to become chief of the War Plans Division and then chief of staff of the army. He immediately immersed himself in efforts to modernize the army and devoted special attention to the growing need for air power. Less than a half year later, in a highly contested race for the coveted position of army chief of staff, President Roosevelt selected Marshall over a pool of more senior general officers.

And so it was on September 1, 1939, the same day that Germany invaded Poland—an action that caused England and France to declare war on Germany—that George Marshall became chief of staff of an army that was outmanned by Germany by a ratio of 30 to 1.

Although he had little background or training in strategic planning or international relations, Marshall understood that the time had come for America to think beyond continental protection, and he took it upon himself to begin pushing the president to prepare the nation for a global war.

Marshall next channeled his energies toward Congress. Like many Americans of the era, a majority of congressmen embraced isolationism. They viewed America's involvement in World War I as a horrendous mistake and were intent on keeping the United States out of the current European situation. It fell to Marshall to move the isolationist, risk-averse body to action.

In early 1940, with the outbreak of major combat across the globe, Marshall redoubled his efforts. As the crisis deepened, he helped institute the first-ever peacetime draft. He removed hundreds of senior army officers whom he felt were no longer up to the physical and intellectual rigors of modern warfare and promoted in their stead scores of promising junior officers. He improved cooperation between the army and navy and began laying the foundation for closer Allied cooperation.

In addition to these many significant but relatively quiet accomplishments, Marshall balanced his responsibilities for training and building a modern army with the demands of meeting the material needs of Great Britain and the Soviet Union—since both countries were in the midst of a historic struggle with Germany and required American equipment and supplies to wage war.

Then, in the summer of 1941, in the face of a hostile Congress and American public, Marshall played a critical role in extending the draft and thus keeping hundreds of thousands of men in the military. It was an act that soon proved essential to America's security when Japan attacked America only months later.

The Global Strategist

Marshall's job only increased in scope and magnitude with the declaration of war. Faced with a truly global conflict, it fell to Marshall to make vital decisions on a daily basis regarding the movement of U.S. troops and the allocation of precious supplies and equipment. For instance, while General MacArthur, the U.S. Navy, and Chiang Kai-shek clamored for more resources to fight the Japanese in the Pacific, General Eisenhower and the British argued that more attention needed to be devoted to Europe.

It was during this period that Marshall began to confront the powerful personalities of Roosevelt and Churchill. With Roosevelt, he slowly maneuvered the skillful politician away from a belief that air power alone could defeat Germany and pointed to the unforgiving reality that the war in Europe could only end with a massive battle—fought by large armies—on the continent. Marshall also had to bring Churchill and Britain's other wartime leaders—who had witnessed the loss of an entire generation of men on the battlefields of Europe in World War I—to the same dire conclusion about the necessity of attacking Germany on the European continent. Diplomatically but firmly, he weaned the British from an approach that favored bombing, naval blockades, and peripheral attacks in the Mediterranean as the primary method for defeating Germany.

Although it took the better part of two years, Marshall countered every possible argument and ultimately succeeded in getting the Allied leaders to agree to his strategic vision. His persistence on a "Germany-first" strategy literally "changed the course of history," and today he is recognized as the architect of the final strategy. It was among his greatest accomplishments of the war.

In 1943, a year when Roosevelt, Churchill, and Joseph Stalin were slowly reversing years of retreats and defeats with offensive action, *Time* chose instead to honor General George C. Marshall as its Man of the Year. In so doing, the magazine's editors said that Marshall was "the closest thing to 'the indispensable man'" and more trusted than "any military man since George Washington." They also said that he was responsible for America actualizing her strength—and it was this strength that allowed America and her allies to fully arm themselves and turn the tide of the war.

Time was not alone in its praise. In a poll of news reporters and historians during the same period, *Newsweek* selected George Marshall "as the individual who made the greatest contribution to the nation's leadership." He received one more vote than President Roosevelt.

On to Victory

In the autumn of 1943, as his vision of a cross-channel invasion of Europe was being assembled into an impending reality, Marshall had every right to expect that he would be chosen to lead the greatest army ever assembled into action. And yet it was not to be. President Roosevelt told Marshall that he was too valuable to the overall success of the global war effort and that he "could not sleep with him out of the country." The job went instead to the man Marshall himself had promoted and men-tored—Dwight D. Eisenhower.

On D-Day, Marshall watched with satisfaction as the troops that were trained according to his ideas, led into battle by lead-ers he personally selected, and supplied with equipment that he had the foresight to provide, began their efficient and relentless march toward victory.

When the war in Europe was finally won, *The New York Times* hailed him as the "architect of victory." Winston Churchill praised "the armies he called into being by his own genius" and said that by war's end there was "no one whose good opinion" he valued more than Marshall's.

George Marshall's job was, however, not finished with the defeat of Hitler's regime. He immediately turned his attention to Japan and counseled the new president, Harry Truman, on his decision to employ the atomic bomb to produce a quick end to the Second World War.

After overseeing the successful conclusion of the war—a war in which he transformed a small continental army into the mightiest army in history—President Truman presided over Marshall's retirement ceremony and said of him that he was "the greatest military man that this country ever produced—or any other country for that matter." Thus on November 26, 1945, after nearly forty-four years in uniform, Marshall retired to his beloved estate, Dodona Manor, in Leesburg, Virginia.

From Soldier to Statesman and Peacemaker

It was perhaps the shortest retirement in the history of the United States government. The following day, President Truman, fearing that the civil war under way in China between Chiang Kai-shek's nationalist forces and Mao Tse-tung's communist guerrillas was spiraling out of control, called on the one man who might be able to salvage the situation—General George C. Marshall. Unable to abandon his strong sense of duty, Marshall informed his disappointed wife, who longed for her husband's retirement, that he had accepted the president's request to serve as his personal emissary to China.

Of Marshall's brief time in China, *Time* correspondent Theodore White wrote, "Never since the days of Roman proconsuls has a single individual held in the name of a great republic such personal responsibility for [the] security of its future and frontiers."[3] Marshall, however, had been given an impossible task. One commentator said of his diplomatic mission, "Talleyrand, Metternich, and Castlereagh could not have pulled it off."[4]

Marshall's stature and stock only increased in Truman's eyes, however. Rather than allow him another opportunity at retirement, President Truman, far from disappointed in his efforts, promoted Marshall to secretary of state.

It was a tumultuous period and certainly among the most critical in the history of American foreign affairs. As the only established democratic, economic, and military power to survive the war intact, the United States had inherited vast global responsibilities. And it fell to George Marshall to translate those responsibilities into concrete actions that would secure the peace he, as a soldier, had done so much to win.

It was no easy chore. The world of 1947 was foaming with discontent. Great Britain had been reduced to a shadow of her former self; the citizens of France and Italy flirted seriously with communism; Germany stewed in her rubble and many of her citizens were engaged in a daily battle for survival against the ravages of disease, hunger, and general chaos. To the east, the states of Hungary, Poland, Czechoslovakia, Romania, and Bulgaria struggled under the repressive grip of the USSR. To the south, Greece was straining under assaults from communist insurgents. In the Middle East, Arabs and Jews waged war. In India, Hindus and Muslims struggled for supremacy in their new country. And in Asia, Korea stood divided, France attempted to reassert its influence in Indochina, and a civil war raged in China.

Yet only days after assuming the position of secretary of state, George Marshall had, in the words of Dean Acheson, Marshall's undersecretary, who later replaced him as secretary, "taken hold" of the state department with his usual "calmness, orderliness, and vigor" and began asserting American power with similar skill.

As he had done with the U.S. Army, Marshall quickly reorganized the state department and surrounded himself with the highest-quality staff. It was under his leadership that the Marshall Plan was initiated and passed into law. The plan was breathtaking in size and scope. Aware of how the United States' nonresponse to the European economic crisis of 1929–1931 had contributed to the rise of Adolf Hitler, Marshall recognized that the spread of social disintegration on the European continent could facilitate the rise of communism and play into the Soviet's hands. And he resolved to do something about it.

Significantly, he did not simply advocate more financial aid. He stressed that it was in both Europe's and America's strategic interests that the economic infrastructure of Europe be strengthened. He therefore requested that aid be provided on the condition that the nations of Europe develop a rational, multilateral approach to their common economic problems. He further stressed that the money must mainly be used to increase industrial capacity and expand foreign trade. Marshall felt that this was the only way the vicious cycle of economic despair would be broken.

After he outlined the plan, Marshall then worked vigorously to pass it through Congress. By overwhelming majorities in both houses, the plan was adopted into law and over the period from 1948 through 1952, it helped rebuild Europe's shipping yards, railroads, and water systems and was instrumental in modernizing the manufacturing, pharmaceutical, and aircraft industries. It gave thousands of Europeans the technical expertise to establish new businesses and played an integral role in rebuilding the factories to produce cars and trucks. In essence, the Marshall Plan allowed capitalism to flourish and established the conditions for Europe's economic and political renaissance.

For his heroic efforts, *Time* again named him Man of the Year for 1947, writing that Marshall was "the man who offered hope to those who desperately needed it."

During his two-year stewardship of the State Department from 1947 to 1949, the basis for NATO was also laid, the Berlin airlift crisis was resolved peacefully, and the policy of "containment" was adopted as official U.S. policy. All told, it was an extraordinarily productive period in American diplomacy.

Upon Truman's famous 1948 upset victory over Thomas Dewey, Marshall requested and was allowed to retire by a thankful President Truman. Again, however, his retirement was short-lived. In 1949, he could not say no when he was asked to serve as president of the American Red Cross—an organization dedicated to helping the world recover from the previous decade of war, but which was itself suffering in the aftermath of war. In short order, Marshall reorganized the agency and revitalized its blood bank program.

In 1950, as the war in Korea grew hotter, President Truman once again called Marshall back to government service. This time he asked him to serve as secretary of defense. For the third time in his career, Marshall—who had spent his entire career in the army battling unpreparedness—was asked to oversee the reconstruction of the U.S. Army, which had been allowed to atrophy in the years since the conclusion of World War II. In less than a year, Marshall tripled the strength of the army and used that strength to prosecute a peaceful resolution to the Korean War. Equally important, during his tenure Marshall finally succeeded in creating the framework for a strong defense policy that stressed the best way to *prevent* war was to be *prepared* for war—a policy that still largely exists to this day. And, in one of his final official acts, Marshall helped assert the supremacy of civilian rule when he supported President

Truman in his controversial decision to relieve General Douglas MacArthur of his command in the Pacific.

In September 1951, General of the Army and Secretary of Defense George Catlett Marshall retired for the final time. The world would continue to praise the man "who won the war" in the years that followed. Marshall himself would continue to serve the country's fallen troops as chairman of the American Battle Monument Commission; serve society as board member of the National Geographic Society; and serve the broader world community as a member of the Atlantic Council. But on December 10, 1953, he received his greatest honor when he became the only professional soldier to win the Nobel Peace Prize. In awarding him the honor, the Nobel committee praised his leadership and his role in creating and implementing the Marshall Plan.

By the time he died on October 16, 1959, all he had done, as President Truman once said, "was win the war and keep the peace." For his great accomplishments and for his selfless devotion to duty, persistent dedication, relentless preparation, and farsighted wisdom, George Marshall truly deserves to be called the twentieth century's "indispensable man."

PART II : The Leadership Principles
of George C. Marshall

DOING THE RIGHT THING
The Principle of Integrity

[T]he immensity of his integrity, and the loftiness and beauty of his character . . .
> —Dean Acheson, commenting on what made George Marshall great

I will give you the best I have.
> —George C. Marshall, upon accepting President Franklin
> Delano Roosevelt's invitation to become army chief of staff

★ ★ ★ ★ ★

By mid-1941, in just two years as army chief of staff, George Marshall had already increased the size of the U.S. Army from 175,000 to 1.4 million troops. It was a considerable accomplishment and would have been sufficient if the country were only in need of a military force capable of protecting the continental United States and its interests in the Western Hemisphere. It was wholly inadequate in the event of a global war in which America had to project power abroad—something that Germany's and Japan's growing power and aggressive, expansionist policies portended.

Marshall thus ordered his staff to draw up two separate plans—one for aiding Great Britain and the other for anticipating U.S. involvement in a war with Germany on the European continent. By April, he had concluded that the second option was the more likely scenario and realized he had to "begin the education of the president as to the true strategic situation . . . and tell him what he had to work with."[1]

What Roosevelt had to work with, while dramatically greater than what was available two years earlier, was still far short of what was necessary. Even worse, from Marshall's perspective, was the prospect that a vast majority of the troops who had been drafted into the army the previous year were scheduled to be released from active duty unless a change in the selective service law (which enabled the draft) was made. America appeared to be poised to take a huge step backward at the precise moment it needed to be making a quantum leap forward.

It fell to Marshall to convince the president, Congress, and ultimately the American people that the retention of the draftees indefinitely, while painful, was necessary because of the chaotic and fluid global situation. But Congress, always attentive to public opinion, was in no mood to alienate the men who were clamoring to get out of the army and return to civilian life. And President Roosevelt, who had campaigned against an extension of the draft the previous fall, was equally unwilling to take the lead on the controversial action.

Marshall knew he had to lead and, in spite of receiving hundreds of hate letters and being called everything from "Hitler Marshall" to a "Benedict Arnold," he pressed on in his belief that an extension of the draft was the right thing to do. That summer, in more than a dozen and a half congressional hearings, Marshall stressed that the national interest was imperiled and an emergency existed "whether or not Congress declares it." Marshall even attempted to ease the burden on Congress by stating that he personally believed it was urgently necessary and in the public interest that Congress declare the existence of a national emergency.

In spite of the message and his willingness to shoulder more than his share of responsibility for the act, congressional leaders wavered and looked for ways to avoid accepting responsibility for a decision that, constitutionally, could only be made by them. One longtime congressional aide noted, at the time, that in his forty years on Capitol Hill, "he had never seen such fear of a bill."[2]

Congress continued to play politics with the bill and resorted to various games in an effort to skirt responsibility. In one critical meeting, Marshall explained to a group of forty Republican leaders the necessity of the act. Afterward, a few of them informed Marshall that they had been convinced and would support the measure. One, however, responded by saying, "You put the case very well, but I will be damned if I am going along with Mr. Roosevelt." Stunned by the overt, partisan nature of the response, Marshall, who was normally very respectful of civilian leaders, responded in a cold fury: "You are going to let plain hatred of the personality dictate to you to do something that you realize is very harmful to the interest of the country."

Undeterred by such examples of pettiness, Marshall only grew more determined. At one stage during the debate, certain members of Congress attempted to sneak an amendment onto the legislation that would have had the effect of shifting the responsibility for extending the term of service for the draftees from Congress to the president. (This amendment would have allowed soldiers to be officially discharged and then made the president—and not Congress—the party responsible for calling them back to duty.)

Asked whether he would support the amendment—which would have guaranteed the bill's passage—Marshall refused to take the easy, expedient path, and he responded by saying, "I want to go right straight down the road, to do what is best, and to do it frankly and without evasion." George Marshall was willing to do his duty and take more than his share of the responsibility, but his integrity would not permit him to allow Congress to evade its responsibility—especially at the expense of the president.

The amendment was not accepted. However, in large measure because of Marshall's efforts over the previous months, the overall bill did pass, but only by the narrowest of margins—203 to 202 votes in the House. Thus, by a single vote America avoided the disintegration of its ground and air forces. And as the events at Pearl Harbor would prove only months later, America would need every ounce of its strength. Whether Marshall's countrymen realized it or not at the time, they were indebted to his willingness to "go right straight down the road, to do what is best, and to do it frankly and without evasion." In short, they were indebted to Marshall's willingness to "do the right thing," which constitutes the first of his leadership principles—the principle of integrity.

A Life of Integrity

In 1914, after nearly thirteen years in the army, George Marshall wrote to General Edward Nichols, the commandant of the Virginia Military Institute, and uncharacteristically lamented the "absolute stagnation" in the army and announced his intention to pursue an alternative career. He said that while the opportunity to accept the comfortable life of an officer was tempting—

especially when compared with the prospect of starting life anew at age 34—"acceptance of my present secured position would mean that I lacked the backbone and necessary moral courage to do the right thing."

Nichols urged Marshall to reconsider the matter and reminded him that he was an "eminent success" and "highly esteemed by everyone" who knew him. Marshall listened to the advice. Within five years, he had distinguished himself in service to his country in the First World War just as Nichols predicted.

Shortly after the war, Marshall was approached by a partner of the J. P. Morgan bank and offered a job with a starting annual salary of $30,000—a staggering sum in an era when the average American salary was only $750 and a major in the army made only slightly more. He turned the job offer down.

Marshall never offered an explanation, but the reason for this decision can be found in his earlier letter to Nichols when he spoke of finding the "necessary moral courage to do the right thing." In 1914, in spite of the frustrations of army life, the "right thing" to do was to stay; and in 1919, in spite of the extraordinary monetary offer, staying in the army and serving his country was still the right thing.

In 1916, Marshall served as aide to General J. Franklin Bell on the eve of America's entry into World War I. Shortly after arriving at his new position, Bell fell ill, and Marshall was asked to assume immense responsibilities. Among these was the job of selecting civilians to serve in the U.S. Army Officer Corps. Caught up in the patriotic fervor of the time, a number of prominent, wealthy, and powerful individuals—including former President William Howard Taft and senior executives at J. P.

Morgan—petitioned Marshall to allow their family members and friends to be approved for the three-month officer training course. Marshall later said that they "all seemed to think they could get what they wanted right away." Those who felt this way didn't know George Marshall. He refused to be intimidated by power or corrupted by wealth or money. In the end, he only selected those individuals who qualified on the basis of merit.

After the war, Marshall was assigned to serve as a key aide to General John J. Pershing, who had replaced General Peyton March as the chief of staff of the army. It was well known that the two generals did not like one another. One day, Marshall presented Pershing with a portion of the official history of the U.S. Army in the First World War, and it included a section favorable to March. Pershing slammed his fist down on his desk and told Marshall in no uncertain terms that he was opposed to the description, and told him to rewrite it another way. Unfazed, Marshall stood his ground and replied, "Now. General, just because you hate the guts of General March, you're setting yourself up . . . to do something you know damn well is wrong." Pershing paused, thought about it for a moment, and then conceded. Marshall's integrity won the day.

At Fort Moultrie in South Carolina, Marshall was charged with overseeing a large number of Civilian Conservation Corps (CCC) districts through the southeastern portion of the country. One day, a brash young major stormed into his office and said, "I've put twelve years in the army. I'm a graduate of West Point. I'm not going to come down here and deal with a whole lot of bums . . . [and] half-dead Southern crackers." The major fully expected Marshall to cave to his demands because of the dearth of qualified officers serving in the army at the time. Marshall, however, had been given a responsibility to train the malnourished and undereducated CCC recruits and responded by replying, "Major, I'm sorry you feel like that. But I'll tell you this—you can't resign quick enough to suit me." The major was stunned. Without giving him a chance to reconsider, Marshall then added, "Now get out of here!" In his book, no one was above accepting his responsibilities.

Incorruptible Power

Lord Acton once said, "Power corrupts, and absolute power corrupts absolutely." While history has shown there is a strong element of truth in the statement, it did not apply to George Marshall. Shortly after receiving his first star and becoming commander of a brigade of the Third Army in Washington, a group of African-American CCC enrollees rebelled against their officers. Marshall had it within his power to crush the insurrection and punish the men. Instead, he assembled the group and acknowledged their concerns by stating, "You feel you been discriminated against on account of your color." He then informed them why they were wrong to take matters into their hands and told them that "[a]s I stand before you here I do not see the pigmentation of your flesh." He went on to assure them that his decision regarding their actions would rest solely on the merits of the case. So successful was Marshall in demonstrating his fairness that when he was done, "the enrollees, to a man, rose and cheered."[3]

Even the ascension to the army's highest office didn't change him. After he was appointed as chief of staff, Louis Johnson, then assistant secretary of war and a top supporter of Marshall in the race to win this post, chided Marshall for not supporting him in his bid to become secretary of war over the incumbent, Harry Woodring. "Listen, Mr. Secretary," Marshall responded, "I was appointed chief of staff and I think you had something to do with it. But Mr. Woodring was secretary of war, and I owed loyalty to him." He then added, "I can't expect loyalty from the army if I do not give it." In Marshall's book, neither friendship nor favoritism had a place in making decisions.[4]

Marshall even went to great lengths to prevent himself from falling prey to the allures of power. He had always refused to vote because he subscribed to the belief that a professional soldier should remain above politics, but he took a number of other steps to insulate himself from the corrupting influence of power once he became chief of staff. For instance, he declined invitations to drop by the White House for drinks with the president and never once accepted the president's offer to visit his estate in Hyde Park for a weekend. He even refused to laugh at the president's jokes. Such rigid policies may seem out of place today, but Marshall employed them as an extra layer of defense for ensuring his integrity was never pierced. He did not want to become intoxicated by the perks of power or allow personal fondness for the president to cloud his judgment.

Doing the Right Thing

When the time came to prepare the officer corps for war, Marshall's integrity demanded that American troops be provided the ablest and most competent officers. Neither seniority, political influence, nor friendship was going to stop him from achieving this end. In addition to relieving hundreds of older officers, Marshall did not hesitate to tell old friends they would also have to resign. In fact, Marshall once ordered a friend overseas for an important post. He soon learned that his friend had said he couldn't leave for a month because his wife was away. Marshall confronted the man, who confirmed the story was true, and replied, "My God, man, we are at war and you are a general." When the friend apologized, Marshall responded, "I'm sorry, too, but you will be retired tomorrow."[5]

Marshall's integrity was also evident in how he treated all people—regardless of gender or race. In 1941, when legislation permitting the use of women in the army was introduced, Marshall was one of the few officers to greet it "with enthusiasm rather than apprehension." An aide of his later said that Marshall supported the bill because he had "a passionate regard for democratic ideals." Marshall felt that if women wanted to serve in the army they should be afforded the same opportunity as a man.

Marshall also gave his full support to the Reserve Officer's Training Corps and the pilots' training programs at the Tuskegee Institute—a program designed to train black military officers. He even made a cash donation to the Institute, which caused the head of the school to write, "I am almost embarrassed by your generous contribution . . . for I regard you as already one of our benefactors."

Marshall's integrity continued to shine even in his last official job. Early during his short tenure as secretary of defense, his appointment for assistant secretary of defense, Anna Rosenberg, came under attack by Joseph McCarthy and his allies in the

Senate during her confirmation hearings. Marshall stood by her side and declared, "We will fight this together." He then enlisted the help of Dwight Eisenhower and others to win over reluctant Republican senators. Later, after she was confirmed, Rosenberg argued with him about fully integrating blacks into fighting units in Korea, which Marshall initially opposed on the grounds that the army—especially during a war—was not the proper place to implement social policy. To his credit, Marshall listened to her arguments, and when she had convinced him, he had the courage and the integrity to change his mind.

The "Aura" of Integrity

Unlike Douglas MacArthur with his famous corncob pipe, or George Patton with his ivory-handled pistol, Marshall neither looked nor acted like a prima donna. He did not feel compelled to sport superfluous military ribbons on his chest, and except for the four-star (later five-star) insignia on his collar, Marshall wore nothing that caused him to stand out. Still, legions of officers who served under him commented on his physical presence and his aura. These traits were not, however, born of toughness, showmanship, or even past battlefield experience; rather, they were the product of his integrity. Marshall's willingness to do the right thing made him an intimidating force in his own right. The legendary George Patton once said, "I would have rather faced the whole Nazi panzer division alone than have an interview with General Marshall."

Likely, Marshall would have been somewhat embarrassed by the comment, and he may have even recognized that his aura could be counterproductive if it caused subordinates to avoid him out of fear or intimidation. Instead, his integrity seems to have driven those around him to want to meet and exceed his high expectations. Upon Marshall's retirement, General Walter Bedell Smith wrote him a short letter that captured this sentiment when he said he would continue trying to meet Marshall's high standards "as long as I live."

Marshall's integrity helped him get the most out of his people, and it yielded a number of other positive side effects. For instance, Marshall's extraordinary relationship with Congress was based in large part on his integrity. Speaker of the House Sam Rayburn once said of Marshall that congressmen always knew that when he was testifying before them, they were "in the presence of a man who is telling us the truth, as he sees it." Rayburn added that Marshall would "tell the truth even if it hurt his cause." This trust was instrumental in Congress granting him a $100 million discretionary fund to expedite expenditures that were either deemed immediately necessary or, alternatively, so sensitive that even Congress could not be allowed to know that the army was working on them. It was out of these funds that the Manhattan Project was initiated.

Moreover, it was Marshall's integrity that lay at the heart of his ability to get the president, the Congress, and the American people to take necessary, albeit difficult, actions. And that is one of the interesting things about people of integrity—they also expect and demand it of others. After the war, Marshall was one of a small minority of leaders who understood the full scope and scale of the global responsibility that had befallen the United States as a result of its victory in the war. He understood his fellow Americans had to "face up to the vast responsibility" that history had clearly placed upon the country and support the effort to rebuild Europe. Marshall refused to sugarcoat (for either Congress or the American people) the fact that his plan would require short-term sacrifice in order to achieve long-term prosperity.

Such was his integrity—and the respect that it commanded—that even though less than half of all Americans had heard of the Marshall Plan, and only one in seven could articulate its goals, the public accepted it and its proposed price tag of $17 billion. A majority of Americans would have preferred to keep the money at home, but they accepted the plan because George Marshall said it was necessary, and they took him at his word.

Lessons: In His Own Words

"[Find] the necessary moral courage to do the right thing." Marshall demonstrated his willingness to do the right thing when he demanded the resignation of the army officer who refused to work with the poor, uneducated civilians in the CCC. A modern example of such integrity can be found in the example that Bill George, former CEO of Medtronic, recounts in his book *Authentic Leadership*. During an audit of one of Medtronic's foreign divisions, a bogus contract was found. When George confronted the division president, he was told that the contract was essential for "doing business" in Italy. (In essence, the contract was used to hide funds, which were used for bribes.) When George pressed the division president about

the fund, he was told, "You don't want to know about that fund." George responded that he did. Upon learning the truth, George told the division president that he had violated Medtronic's values and must "resign immediately."[6] George refused to allow past practices or profits to prevent him from doing the right thing.

Coleen Rowley, the mid-level FBI agent who confronted the FBI director with information that the agency had ignored pleas from field agents that could have been used to possibly prevent the attacks of 9/11, demonstrated similar moral courage. She took action, even though as her family's sole breadwinner and only two and a half years away from retirement, she could have faced retribution.

Such action need not occur only at the executive level. In 2002, Elizabeth Joice, a high school teacher in Peoria, Arizona, failed one of her senior students. The consequence was that he would not be allowed to graduate. The student's parents hired a lawyer and attempted to intimidate Joice. She stood her ground. Unfortunately, the school district ultimately caved into the pressure and rescinded the decision; nonetheless, Joice had still sent a powerful message to her students—especially those who had legitimately passed her course—that she had attempted to fulfill her rightful obligation to assess students on the basis of their classroom performance.[7]

Amo Houghton, former CEO of Corning Glass Works and currently a U.S. congressman, often tells the story of his predecessor's advice prior to taking the helm of the company. "Think of your decisions [as] being based on two concentric circles," he counseled. "In the outer circle are all the laws, regulations, and ethical standards with which the company must comply. In the inner circle are your core values. Just be darn sure that your decision as CEO stays within your inner circle." It was advice that George Marshall would have well understood.

"I want to go right straight down the road, to do what is best, and do it frankly and without evasion." George Marshall voiced these words in the midst of a heated debate over the issue of extending the draft in the summer of 1941. He had been presented with a politically expedient amendment that would have allowed the bill to pass into law, but he had refused to accept it because it would have amounted to a semiethical trick.

In May 2004, Gap Inc. released a forty-page "social responsibility report" that succinctly and honestly described a series of wage, health, and safety violations in its overseas manufacturing plants. Rather than gloss over or hide the violations, Gap Inc. laid its violations out for the public to see. The report outlined goals for the following year and created an external review of its own monitoring system. It is too soon to tell whether Gap Inc. will correct all of its problems, but it has taken a substantial step in the right direction by truthfully acknowledging and striving to deal with them in a forthright manner.[8]

Another good example of "going straight down the road," occurred in 2003, when General Eric Shinseki testified before the Senate Armed Forces Committee on the issue of Iraq (before America had gone to war). When questioned about the number of troops needed to keep the peace after the war, Shinseki said, "Something on the order of several hundred thousand." It was not a number his immediate superior, Secretary of Defense

Donald Rumsfeld, wanted to hear, but, as recent history suggests, it was much closer to the mark.

Shinseki's testimony had nothing to do with his personal feelings over the wisdom of going to war. He provided his honest assessment of the situation because he understood that if too few troops were provided, the soldiers who were sent to Iraq would be placed in greater danger and the long-term prospects for success would be diminished. Shinseki never forgot that his first loyalty was to tell the "difficult truths," protect his troops, and win the war. It was not his job to parrot the views of his civilian superiors for the sake of political expediency.

Coleen Rowley did the same thing with her memo to the FBI director. She understood that her job was to protect the American people—not the image of the FBI. As Bill George once said, "Integrity is not just the absence of lying, but telling the whole truth, as powerful as it may be."[9]

"I can't afford the luxury of sentiment." George Marshall admitted that firing old acquaintances was one of the most difficult aspects of his job, but he never failed to do it when necessary because he understood that the interests of the organization always came before his own interests. Ram Charan, in his book *Execution: The Discipline of Getting Things Done* (written with Larry Bossidy), tells of the CEO of a large company who was unable to fire an "old and trusted colleague." The CEO was unable to do it, even though he knew the old friend was failing. The situation was made even worse because the friend was responsible for close to 60 percent of the company's business. Ultimately, the CEO lost his job, but not before he cost the

company millions of dollars in losses and painful layoffs.[10] People of integrity understand that even actions that are personally difficult must be taken if they jeopardize the health or good standing of the organization they work for.

For instance, shortly after Peter I. Bijur, the CEO of Texaco in the late 1990s, took over the helm of the company, it was sued for racial discrimination. A few weeks later, an audiotape documenting senior executives making derogatory racial remarks was revealed. Bijur immediately acknowledged the problem, fired the executives who made the racist remarks, and settled the lawsuit. Bijur then set about changing the culture of the company and hired a number of prominent African-Americans. Today, Chevron Texaco is widely praised as a model for reducing discrimination in the workplace.[11]

"Do [your] convincing within the team." As chief of staff, Marshall always offered his advice in private and never once went around the president's back with his disagreements to the press. As he said, "I thought that it was far more important in the long run that I be well established as a member of the team and try to do my convincing within that team, than to take action publicly contrary to the desires of the president and certain members of Congress."

Intel Corporation has a similar policy. It is called *disagree and commit.* The policy actively encourages people to openly and freely disagree with proposed policies or actions, but if the person is overruled (after his arguments have been heard and considered) he is expected to fully commit to the idea.

"I can't expect loyalty from the army if I do not give it." This was Marshall's response to a civilian superior who supported him in his quest to become chief of staff of the army, and later asked him to support him in his bid to become the secretary of war. Marshall refused because it would have been disloyal to the then-current secretary of war.

The same integrity was demonstrated by Ed Breen when he was selected to replace Dennis Kozlowski as the CEO of Tyco International in the wake of Kozlowski's indictment for tax evasion and stock fraud in 2002. It would have been easy for Breen to retain the same board of directors that had hired him. Instead, he replaced them. He took the action because he wanted to send a message to the public and the market that Tyco was going to be a different type of company. Breen understood that his loyalty was to Tyco shareholders and the broader public, not the board that had hired him.

"I do not want anything to be done that would not be done for Tom, Dick, or Harry . . . I must not be put in the position of backing favorites in my own family." This was the message that Marshall sent to the commanding officer of one of his stepsons when he suspected that that officer might be considering giving preference to a member of his family. Marshall's act is not dissimilar to the policies of DuPont and the British firm J. Lyons & Company. In both instances, family members are given entry-level jobs, but they are only promoted if a panel of nonfamily members judges them superior to their peers in terms of performance, knowledge, and future potential.[12]

"We will stick this out." These were the words Marshall said to Anna Rosenberg, the first women ever nominated for a senior position with the Defense Department, when she was attacked by Joseph McCarthy and wrongly accused of being a communist. Marshall never wavered in his support for her and, in the end, helped get her confirmed. Thomas Kean, the former governor of New Jersey and the co-chairman of the 9/11 Commission, demonstrated a similar level of support when he defended Jamie Gorelick, a Democratic member of his committee, against partisan attacks during the investigation. Kean's integrity went a long way toward creating an atmosphere where all the members—Republicans and Democrats alike—were able to freely express themselves without fear of recrimination. Kean's support was also instrumental in creating a truly bipartisan report that outlined a number of substantive recommendations for improving America's intelligence program.

"There must be no friend of mine on the board." These were Marshall's instructions to his civilian superiors when Congress in 1944 required army and navy boards to investigate America's failure at Pearl Harbor. In the 1970s, Kenneth Dayton, former chairman of Dayton Hudson (now Target Corporation), fundamentally reorganized his company's board of directors. Among the more revolutionary aspects Dayton incorporated was the requirement that a substantial majority of the board be independent directors. He also created a governance committee and mandated that the board regularly evaluate the CEO. At the time, Dayton's moves were considered radical, but the depth, perspective, and experience of a more independent board have

allowed the company to survive hostile takeover bids, economic downturns, and CEO changes over the years.

"You have my complete authority to do what your judgment tells you is right . . ." These were the instructions Marshall once gave a subordinate. He undoubtedly expressed the same sentiment to scores of other people over the course of his long career.

It is unlikely that Kenneth Lay, former CEO of Enron, ever issued the same instruction to his employees. For if he had, it is doubtful the executives under him—not to mention the junior Enron traders who manipulated the California energy system for their own gain—would have acted the way they did. Integrity starts at the top, and if it isn't demonstrated, it should not come as a surprise when subordinates also demonstrate a lack of it.

Betsy Bernard, the former president of AT&T, once offered this advice that was given to her by a former chairman:

> In whatever organization you find yourself, remember that people talk. And it's not all idle gossip. Our cultures learn to protect themselves by getting the word around about people whose honor is doubtful. You'll never be more valuable than your word.

> I don't mean this as a warning, but as an opportunity—because, by the same token, healthy organizations also spread the word about people of incorruptible honesty. So tell the truth, deliver what you promise, let your caring show, and you'll be noticed. In fact, they're searching for you right now.[13]

The Way to Go

In 1932, as the head of instruction at the Army Infantry School at Fort Benning, Georgia, Marshall oversaw the training of regular army officers as well as numerous National Guard and reserve officers. One day, he was presented with a petition by a group of white officers demanding that two black reserve officers training at the facility be removed. It would have been easy for Marshall to simply adopt a "go along to get along" philosophy. (After all, he was in a remote post in Georgia and serving in an officer corps of the regular army, which was segregated at the time.) Instead, he denied the petition outright and allowed the two black officers to stay.

In so many ways, Marshall's act mirrors the recent actions of Sherron Watkins and Cynthia Cooper. Watkins, when she was a vice president at Enron, had the courage to write Kenneth Lay a letter and warn him about improper accounting practices. Cooper demonstrated similar integrity when, as WorldCom's auditor, she bravely informed the company's board that its executives were committing fraud on a massive scale.

Christopher Patten, the former governor of Hong Kong, once gave a keynote speech honoring George Marshall, and he concluded his remarks by quoting the end of his favorite novel, *Middlemarch*, by George Eliot. It reads, in part:

> The growing good of the world is partly dependent on unhistoric acts, and that things are not so ill with you and me as they might have been, is half owing to the number who lived faithfully a hidden life . . .

The passage is a reminder that it is the sum total of the thousands of "unhistoric" acts of integrity that ultimately make the world a better place. And every day, there are legions of people quietly performing unhistoric acts: CEOs who are forgoing short-term gains for long-term growth; middle managers who are refusing to engage in unethical behavior solely to advance professionally or monetarily; teachers who are refusing to advance undeserving students; and civil servants who refuse to cater to the demands of powerful, partisan politicians.

These individuals may not be immediately recognized, but eventually, people of integrity do get noticed. Watkins and Cooper—along with Coleen Rowley of the FBI—were *Time* magazine's people of the year in 2002. Even George Marshall's small act in the backwaters of rural Georgia was eventually recognized. Years later, one of the black officers wrote to him and said, "Your quiet and courageous firmness . . . has served to uphold my belief in the eventual solution of problems which have beset my people in their . . . attempts to be Americans."

The actions of Watkins, Cooper, Rowley, and George Marshall (and thousands of others) demonstrate that whether the problem is large or small, solutions do exist and can be found—but only if people are first willing to act with integrity.

MASTERING THE SITUATION

The Principle of Action

The burden he bore was greater than that of Churchill or Roosevelt, because Marshall was the man who turned policy, mere ideas, into men and steel, into fact.

—Lance Morrow

—Get action where action [is] needed.

—George C. Marshall

* * * * *

As a young boy, Marshall and a childhood friend built a raft to ferry their classmates across a small creek that separated their neighborhood from the local school. The two boys charged a modest fee and, in return, the passengers received a ticket and were transported across the narrow stretch of water. One day, a rebellious group of girls refused to surrender their tickets and began jeering at Marshall, who was acting as the ticket collector. Humiliated and feeling "stuck," Marshall spied a cork on the floor of the boat. "With the inspiration of the moment," he recalled years later, he "pulled the cork and, under the pressure of the weight of the passengers, a stream of water shot up in the air. All the girls screamed and I sank the boat in the middle of the stream . . . I never forgot that because I had to do something and I had to think quickly. What I did set me up again as the . . . master of the situation."

The story captures the essence of Marshall's second leadership principle—mastering the situation—the principle of action.

Man Is Made for Action: A History of Action

In the late-nineteenth century, there was a famous case at the U.S. Military Academy where an officer had been given "a silence" by the men under his command. The act was considered mutinous because it sought to undermine the authority of the officer. In fact, it was deemed so serious that Congress undertook an investigation of the matter. The cadets of the Virginia Military Institute (VMI), where Marshall attended college, were well aware of the incident and early during Marshall's tenure as first captain—VMI's highest-ranking cadet position—they decided to test the mettle of their new leader by falling into a complete silence during an evening meal. The hall soon became so quiet that there was no mistaking it as a deliberate act.

Marshall instantly recognized the silence as a challenge to his leadership. With no hesitation, he called the entire body to attention and marched them out of the mess hall. It was his good fortune that at the time of the incident the cadets had just been served a dessert of fresh strawberries—a rare delicacy in the Spartan-like existence of VMI—and Marshall's prompt action deprived them of their strawberries. More important, the act gained the respect and admiration of his peers and set him up once again as the "master of the situation."

In the spring of 1901, Marshall, not yet a graduate of VMI and not quite twenty-one years old, presented himself at the office of the president of the United States, William McKinley, to press his case for being allowed to take the examination to earn a commission in the United States Army (at the time only graduates of the U.S. Military Academy at West Point were guaranteed a commission). The White House butler informed Marshall that because he didn't have an appointment he would not get in. Still, Marshall patiently waited. Finally, hours later, Marshall mustered up the courage to attach himself to a father and daughter team who had an appointment with the president and surreptitiously gained entry to McKinley's office. After the father-daughter duo completed their visit, Marshall stayed behind and succinctly stated his case to his would-be commander-in-chief. Later in life, Marshall reflected that his commission in the army "flowed" from the meeting. It can perhaps be argued that the rest of his career (and thus his history) stemmed from his willingness to take this bold action.

After earning his commission, Marshall was sent to the Philippines. One day on a routine march across the island, he led his veteran team of soldiers across a narrow stream. In the middle of the crossing one of the men yelled, "Crocodiles!" In the ensuing panic, Marshall was knocked over and pushed into the mud. He calmly picked himself up, marched up to the bank, and ordered his unit to fall into formation. He then issued a "right shoulder arms" command and marched them back down into the river. When he reached the other side, he ordered his troops back across the river. Safely on the other side, Marshall lined his team up and inspected each man's rifle. When he was done, he ordered them to fall out. He had made his point and, more important, he had reasserted his authority through quick action.

In the mid-1920s, Marshall was sent to China where he commanded about 1,000 troops in Tientsin. It was a turbulent time in China's history, and a number of competing armies, controlled by warlords, jockeyed for control. One day, after a critical shift in these alliances (which then governed the country), a throng of 100,000 Chinese troops were quickly displaced. With nowhere else to go, they descended on Tientsin. The city had no natural defenses, so Marshall ordered his soldiers to take up positions around the city and instructed them to demand that the Chinese soldiers turn over their guns in return for food and the right to enter the city. It was a sheer bluff because the 100,000 Chinese troops could have easily overwhelmed Marshall's troops. His willingness to act, however, was enough to convince the Chinese that the United States meant business, and the situation was diffused with no bloodshed.

Later, as army chief of staff, Marshall was even more resolute in his demand for action. Within hours of war being declared in December 1941, Marshall called his staff together and informed them that "the time was long past when matters could be debated and discussed and carried on ad infinitum." Marshall ordered them to "get action where action was needed." And to the first class of graduates from officer candidate school at Fort Benning in 1941, Marshall offered this warning: "Passive inactivity, because you have not been given specific instructions to do this or to do that, is a serious deficiency."

One of Marshall's favorite sayings was "man is made for action." In both word and deed, he proved it.

"Do Something"

Marshall once told a group of young officers to "step out and do something. What if you do fail?" But he did more than just preach this message, he supported it. During the First World War, Marshall was assigned to investigate an incident in which a number of American soldiers were killed in a clandestine raid. He considered the task "most distasteful," and he informed the general staff that there was no need to continue the investigation because his opinion was unlikely to be changed by any further evidence. When asked by the staff what his opinion was, Marshall replied that the "offensive spirit" demonstrated in the raid should be congratulated and that the "unfortunate result" should not be used as a reason to forgo future offensive operations. In short, Marshall was unwilling to penalize someone for taking action just because the outcome was unfavorable.

Once, after a subordinate burst in on President Franklin Roosevelt in the midst of a dental appointment in order to obtain his signature, the president complained to Marshall. Marshall responded by saying, "When I find people who get things done, I won't fire them." The ability and willingness of individuals to take action was one of the key characteristics he looked for in his subordinates.

Another one of Marshall's favorite subordinates was Lieutenant General Brehon B. Somervell, commander of army service forces. Under Somervell's leadership, the department's unofficial motto was: "We do the impossible immediately. The miraculous takes a little longer." In carrying out his duties, Somervell inevitably rubbed a lot of people the wrong way, but Marshall always backed him up because he acted— and got results. Long after the war, he said of Somervell, "If I went into control in another war, I would start out looking for another General Somervell the very first thing."

But perhaps the best example of Marshall's support of action—and an act that Marshall took great pride in and which contributed significantly to America's successful war efforts—was his role in the development of the jeep. During the early stages of World War II, a representative from the Bantam Motor Car Company approached the transport division of the U.S. Army with a model of an unusual four-wheel-drive vehicle that he described as "a small, low silhouette truck, light enough to be manhandled by its passengers, capable of carrying four or five men." The representative's initial forays into the War Department were met with typical bureaucratic resistance. Eventually, the man reached Walter Bedell Smith—then only a major and secretary of the general staff, but later the head of the Central Intelligence Agency— who instantly understood the potential for the small, low truck and went to visit the "one man in the army who could get action in the War Department"—General Marshall.

So enthusiastic was Smith that he interrupted a meeting Marshall was having with a group of generals to tell him that he had just come across a very useful idea, but had been unable to get any "favorable observers" in the War Department. Marshall listened to Smith make his case for a few minutes and asked, "Well, what do you think of it?" Smith replied, "I think it is good." "Well, do it," replied Marshall, who then made the money available to purchase 1,500 jeeps.

The first jeeps met with such an enthusiastic response that soon a second order was authorized. By the war's end, the U.S. Army possessed over 2.5 million jeeps, and their ease-of-use and maneuverability was widely credited with giving American troops a decided advantage, especially in Europe.

Acting with Energy

After the war, early in his new diplomatic career as secretary of state, Marshall told his staff who were arguing over an issue: "Don't fight the problem, decide it." One member of his staff worried that Marshall's penchant for action—a trait that served him so well in the war—was ill-suited for his new diplomatic responsibilities, where "problems were often not susceptible to an answer" or one action is only slightly "less disagreeable than some other action and probably no action is altogether good."[1]

Marshall persisted in his action-oriented approach and told his staff that "I don't want you fellows sitting around asking me what to do. I want you to tell me what to do." And contrary to the staff member's concern, Marshall's two-year tenure at the State Department was filled with a series of actions that yielded extraordinary results.

In early 1947, Britain informed the United States that it would no longer be able to maintain responsibility for the security of the eastern Mediterranean region—specifically Greece and Turkey. "The job of world leadership, with all its burdens and all its glory," said one official, now fell to the United States.

With communist insurgents attacking the government of Greece, and the Soviet Union hoping to exploit the situation in Turkey, Marshall recognized the seriousness of the situation. In an address to the American public, he warned, "We are at the point of decision."

The decision, Marshall knew, demanded action—and action required money. Specifically, it would cost $400 million. Congress, which was anxious to enact a 20 percent tax cut in the aftermath of the war, initially balked at the price tag. Marshall, however, warned, "The choice is between acting with energy or losing by default." And as it had so many times during the war years, Congress heeded Marshall's call to action and provided the money.

His call, of course, led directly to the creation of the Marshall Plan. After trying to diplomatically resolve the issue of the reconstruction of Western Europe with the Soviet Union, Marshall reluctantly came to the conclusion that the Soviets were not serious, and he declared that "action cannot await compromise through exhaustion."

Later in life, Marshall said that there was nothing terribly profound in the development of the plan, but the aspect he took the most pride in was pushing it through Congress. He said he worked as hard on passing the plan as he would have if he were "running for . . . the presidency." He testified before Congress, worked with the Senate Republican leadership, and laid out the rationale for the program before scores of business, agricultural, and church groups—all in an effort to secure the public's support.

Woodrow Wilson once said, "Those only are leaders of men . . . who lead in action . . . it is at their hands that new thought gets its translation into the crude language of deeds." And, as Lance Morrow more recently noted, George Marshall did precisely that. It was he who turned Roosevelt and Churchill's "mere ideas . . . into fact."[2] Marshall did it, in large part, by having the courage to act. And for that he deserves to be called a great leader.

Lessons: In His Own Words

"Man is made for action." This was one of Marshall's favorite statements. It reflects his strong belief that an imperfect act taken quickly was frequently superior to a "perfect" action taken later.

In 1948, when the Soviet Union blockaded Berlin, Marshall, rather than confronting the Soviets militarily, instead organized the Berlin airlift. It was a somewhat risky act, and although it took the better part of a year, it peacefully resolved the situation. As he had done so many times before, Marshall demonstrated that it wasn't necessarily the size of the act that mattered. Rather, it was the simple fact that an action was taken.

In 1977, Richard Thalheimer saw an ad in a magazine for a solid-state chronograph watch for less than $100. Because the watch was shock resistant and the price was right, he thought the device would be perfect for runners. Undoubtedly, thousands of other people also saw the ad, but only Thalheimer acted. He spoke with the importer of the product and started selling his "jogger's watch" in *Runner's World*. His first ad resulted in $90,000 in sales. He soon began selling other unique, high-tech products through catalogs, and today his

Sharper Image stores are located throughout the United States and his annual sales exceed $400 million.[3]

In his book, *On Becoming a Leader*, Warren Bennis quotes former Lucky Stores executive Don Ritchey, who said: "Even if you're pretty analytical by nature, you have to be willing to make a decision somewhere short of certainty. You just haven't got the time or the resources ... you have to get 80 percent or 85 percent of it and then take your best shot."[4] It is an approach that General Marshall would have well understood—and supported.

"Do it." This was Marshall's simple response to Walter Bedell Smith when he presented him with the idea to manufacture the jeep. In retrospect, the rugged, maneuverable vehicle seems a natural fit for the fluid and swift nature of modern warfare. Yet the idea was consistently rejected by War Department leaders. All it took, however, was a small act of Marshall and one of his staff to get the ball rolling—and the ball didn't stop rolling until 2.5 million jeeps helped influence the outcome of the war.

In 1967, Eleanor Josaitis was a housewife in Detroit when she witnessed race riots that nearly destroyed her hometown. The following year she decided to cofound, along with Father William Cunningham, a food program designed to serve pregnant women, new mothers, and their children. Over time, the organization began helping other individuals join the economic mainstream by offering them a practical education and access to state-of-the-art information technology. Today, Focus: HOPE employs more than 500 people, boasts 50,000 volunteers, and has helped thousands of people become gainfully employed. And it all started because, as Josaitis said, "You have to have the guts to try *something*."[5]

"Do as I say. I will accept all responsibility." In early 1918, Marshall was the chief of G3 (operations) of the First Division in France. Among his responsibilities was issuing orders to the troops in the field. He soon found the process so burdensome and shrouded in secrecy that by the time the orders could be issued they were of limited use to the soldiers. Marshall ordered his subordinates, if necessary, to use the telephone to issue the orders. One officer replied that it "was a direct violation of security." Marshall responded by saying, "Do as I say. I will accept all responsibility."[6] He understood that with American lives at stake, he had to act.

One of the primary things executives and leaders get paid to do is make tough choices. Often these decisions must be made with less than perfect information, under extremely trying conditions, and with no real guide to action. The only thing that a leader can really do is act and take responsibility. Jim Burke, the former CEO of Johnson & Johnson who handled the famous Tylenol tampering case in the early 1980s (seven people died after being poisoned with cyanide-laced pills), offers a real-world example. There was no model for how to act in such a situation, but Burke instinctively knew that the right thing to do was to pull all bottles of Tylenol from store shelves and go on national television to explain everything the company was doing to prevent more deaths and thwart future problems. He took these actions against the advice of his head of public relations, who claimed that going on *60 Minutes* was "the worst decision that anyone in the company had ever made" because it risked the future financial success of the company. Burke, of course, did it anyway, and Johnson & Johnson actually came out of the crisis stronger and with a better public image because of his willingness to act.[7]

Larry Johnson tells a similar story in his book *Absolute Honesty*. Once he arrived after midnight at a Marriott Hotel. He was very hungry, but he was informed that the kitchen had closed for the night. The clerk, however, soon arrived at his room with a large platter of food. The next morning Johnson asked the manager if the clerk had broken any rules. The manager replied, "You bet he did, but here at Marriott our people are encouraged to break the rules if it's for the right reasons. All we ask is that they use good judgment."[8]

"Step out and do something. What if you do make a mistake?" Marshall loved to see initiative in his subordinates and often went out of his way to praise bold action, even when it failed. A few years ago, the drug Gleevec was "languishing" in Novartis labs when it came to the attention of CEO Dan Vasella. He overcame internal opposition and ordered accelerated clinical trials for the drug. The drug proved so effective that the Food and Drug Administration approved it in record time. Today, it classifies as a "blockbuster" drug and has substantially bolstered Novartis's profits and helped thousands of patients deal with chronic myeloid leukemia.[9] The drug—as many clinical drugs do—could have failed. Vasella, however, refused to allow the fear of failure to prevent him from taking an action he deemed necessary.

Roberto Goizueta, the late CEO of The Coca-Cola Company who successfully introduced Diet Coke, was once told by a former boss that he was "too much a man of action." Goizueta responded by quoting the poet Antonio Machado, who wrote, "Paths are made by walking." Goizueta lived by that philosophy and, as he demonstrated with his infamous decision to create New Coke, sometimes mistakes are made.

Jim Copeland, retired CEO of Deloitte & Touche, tells the story of initially rejecting a business plan presented by a partner because it was "off market and off strategy." When the partner persisted, Copeland still felt it was off market and off strategy but agreed it was a solid business plan. He therefore invested $250,000 in the new venture. Within two years, the business returned $2 million in cash, and the following year it was sold for $50 million. A very healthy return for a small act, and it occurred because Copeland wasn't afraid to fail.[10]

Johnson & Johnson's former CEO, Jim Burke, tells one of the best stories about this lesson. Early in his career he produced a product that failed miserably. He was called in to see the CEO, who declared in a loud voice, "I understand you lost over a million dollars." Burke, thinking he was about to be fired, admitted that he had. The CEO then did something completely unexpected. He offered his hand to Burke and said, "I just want to congratulate you. All business is making decisions, and if you don't make decisions, you won't have any failures." His unstated point, of course, was that without decisions there also wouldn't be any successes. Burke's boss said he was keeping him, in part because he knew Burke would learn from his mistakes. More important, he was keeping Burke because he had finally found someone willing to step up and make a decision. In short, he found someone willing to act.[11]

"[T]he choice is between acting with energy or losing by default." This was Marshall's admonishment to the American public after he became convinced the Soviet Union was not interested in helping Europe recover from the devastation of the Second World War and instead hoped to capitalize on the continuing chaos to promote communism. The advice seems quite obvious—especially today—when the increasing pace of technological advancement and global competitiveness are ever-present realities. Still, in industries large and small, companies continue to play by yesterday's rules and often refuse to take even simple action. In the late 1980s, Bethlehem Steel (which was voted a "best-managed company" by *BusinessWeek* in 1989) refused to address the changes mini-steel manufacturers were introducing, and by 2001, it was bankrupt. In the early 1990s, Robert Stempel, then CEO of General Motors, refused to transform his company and instead continued to manufacture scores of different car models. By 1996, GM's market share had fallen from a high of 44 percent in 1987 to under 32 percent.

Today, many in the energy industry continue to dismiss solar cell and fuel cell technologies. A number of advances in the field of materials sciences are poised to significantly improve these technologies, and if the conventional gas, oil, and nuclear energy industries refuse to deal with these emerging technologies, they very well could risk "losing by default."

"If I find you doing something, I will help you, but if I find you doing nothing, only God will help you." In 1933, while at Fort Moultrie, Marshall oversaw a number of Civilian Conservation Corps (CCC) camps throughout the southeastern United States. Aware that the job of supervising civilians was something new to most army officers under his command, Marshall warned against discouragement and promised support. His support, however, was conditional: "I'll be out to see you soon," he said, "and if I find you doing something, I will help you, but if I find you doing nothing, only God will help you." Marshall's point was clear: He expected his subordinates to act.

Noel Tichy, in his book *The Leadership Engine*, recounts a story about an exchange between two executives at Ameritech (now part of SBC Communications). One day, a vice president at the company mentioned to a general manager that the CEO was coming to visit his plant. The general manager responded by notifying his team the CEO "was coming." The VP later asked the GM why he felt it was necessary to inform his people of the CEO's visit. The message being sent, he said, was that his team only had to be on the ball when the CEO was around. He then chastised the GM for behaving as though he worked in a "bureaucratic society." The vice president, like Marshall, expected action from his people at all times.[12]

"When I find people who get things done, I won't fire them." This was Marshall's response to President Roosevelt when he complained about the aggressive behavior of one of Marshall's subordinates. People of action are, unfortunately, all too rare. President Abraham Lincoln had to go through four commanding generals

before he found Ulysses S. Grant. But when he found Grant, his orders to him were short and simple: "I neither ask nor desire to know anything of your plans. Take responsibility and act, and call me for assistance." The operative word in the statement was "act."

"I am not interested in the explanation . . . I am interested in the result." Near the end of World War II, the American army was achieving spectacular gains in its battle against Germany. Marshall complained to his public relations staff that American troops were not receiving proper recognition. In response, the staff handed him a slew of press releases as proof of their attempt to address his concern. Marshall replied: "My comment on this is that I am not interested in the explanation. What I am interested in [is] the result." What he was saying was that he wanted more action—effective action.

In another instance, Marshall grew concerned about the casualty rates U.S. troops were suffering in the jungles of the Pacific, and he ordered one of his staff to determine what could be done with existing weapons to improve their plight. He added that he didn't want to hear about "something that took a year to produce." Within a few days, modified equipment was being shipped to the Pacific.

Throughout business and life, a significant number of people, when questioned about why a problem hasn't been resolved, respond with an explanation or, worse, offer an excuse instead of simply making a commitment to more effective action. This could be construed as a human failing, but it is the leader's job to prompt the unresponsive party to action—or relieve them if they prove incapable.

In 1992, Tom Tiller, then an executive at General Electric Company, took over a money-losing manufacturing plant. One of his first acts was to take a group of employees on a reconnaissance mission to an annual trade show where they could review the latest equipment and size up their competition. Tiller said the trip "came from a sense of 'Somebody's got to do something here, and we can either wait for them to take care of it, or we can do it ourselves'." Within eighteen months, Tiller's team had "designed, built, and delivered to market" three new products, and the plant had been transformed from a $10 million loss to a $35 million profit.[13]

The Way to Go

Upon his arrival in the Philippines as a freshly minted second lieutenant, Marshall learned that he had been assigned to the island of Mindoro, many miles south of Manila Bay. To get there he had to embark on a small, 250-ton freighter. After waiting for five days in the bay (at the time, captains had to quarantine people for a period to prevent the spread of cholera), the captain ignored typhoon warnings and set sail. Soon after, the ship ran into the "damnedest typhoon you ever saw," according to Marshall. The storm pitched the small ship back and forth so violently that the upper deck would roll to the edge of the water and then teeter on the brink of capsizing before pitching wildly to the other side. Frightened and fearing for his life, the ship's captain left the bridge and cowered in his wardroom.

Marshall seized control of the helm and at gunpoint ordered the engine room to keep up steam. Then, together with another officer, they battled the storm for hours. Although he was not a sailor and he knew even less about handling a ship—especially in the middle of a typhoon—Marshall did the only thing he could, he acted. The story demonstrates that a person does not have to be an expert or even have experience to lead. A person does, however, have to act and, as Marshall's life demonstrates, a great many "typhoons" can be weathered if a person simply has the courage to do something.

SERVING THE GREATER GOOD
The Principal of Selflessness

Most men are slaves of their ambition. General Marshall is the slave of his duties.

—U.S. Senator Richard Russell

The issue was simply too great for any personal feeling to be involved.

—Marshall reflecting on his refusal to ask President Roosevelt

for the command of the Normandy invasion

—

* * * * *

In August 1997, Lance Morrow, a professor at Boston University, wrote a wonderful article entitled "George C. Marshall: The Last Great American?" for *Smithsonian*. In the article he sketched out in the reader's mind a parallelogram of famous military generals named "George"—George Washington and George Marshall; George Armstrong Custer and George Patton. The latter two "Georges," while unquestionably talented, were "martial peacocks," he wrote, for whom "the battle was essentially a dramatically amplified projection of themselves." George Washington and George Marshall, however, he described as "soldiers of maturity and gravitas" who evolved "beyond ego . . . to a sort of higher self-effacement, an identification by which they merged themselves with their country's purpose." The Greeks, he wrote, would have assigned Washington and Marshall to "the realm of *arete*"—or a state of virtue in which an individual finds fulfillment in noble service to his state.[1]

This phrase "realm of areté" accurately captures the essence of the third leadership principle of George C. Marshall: serving the greater good—the principle of selflessness. His life is replete with examples of his selflessness, many of which are recounted in this chapter, but a single example stands out: his refusal to ask President Franklin D. Roosevelt for the one command he truly coveted—the right to lead American and Allied forces in the D-Day invasion.

In late 1943, at the height of World War II, after Marshall had convinced a reluctant Roosevelt and then persuaded an equally stubborn Winston Churchill of the necessity of a cross-channel attack on Germany, the vital question of who would lead Operation Overlord (or what has become more widely known as the D-Day invasion) arose. By almost every standard—seniority, knowledge, experience, and skill—Marshall had the right to expect he would be the man to lead the U.S. Army into its greatest battle in its greatest war.

Roosevelt knew that Marshall was the best man for the job. He knew Marshall wanted the command. He even knew what the decision meant for Marshall in historical terms. When he was considering appointing Marshall to the prestigious command, Roosevelt said to Eisenhower:

> Ike, you and I know who was chief of staff during the last years of the Civil War, but practically no one else knows, although the names of Grant, Lee, and Jackson . . . every schoolboy knows them. I hate to think that fifty years from now practically nobody will know who George Marshall was. That

is one of the reasons why I want George to have the big command. He is entitled to establish his place in history as a great general.

Yet, when the time came to make the decision, Roosevelt balked. He balked because he understood how vital Marshall was to the overall war effort. Marshall, alone among his army peers—including Dwight D. Eisenhower and Douglas MacArthur—had a commanding view of the world situation. And among his other senior military advisers, only Marshall had the ability to stand up to the powerful personalities of Churchill, Joseph Stalin, Charles de Gaulle, and Chiang Kai-shek.

Roosevelt was thus in a quandary. He knew Marshall deserved and wanted the job, but he also understood Marshall was too valuable to limit his talents to one theater of the war—no matter how big or important that theater might be. Luckily for America—but unfortunately for Marshall—the wily and instinctive president played the one card that could get him out of his predicament: Marshall's own selflessness. Roosevelt decided to offer Marshall the command on the sole condition that he ask for it.

The president had accurately sized up the general. Marshall was too duty-bound to ask for anything for himself. He responded to Roosevelt's offer by simply saying, "I will serve wherever you order me, Mr. President." To emphasize his point, Marshall added that the president should "feel free to act in . . . the best interest of the country" and not "in any way consider my feelings."

Thus did the command of the Normandy invasion—one of Marshall's "deepest hopes" and one of history's surest invitations to glory and immortality—slip from his hands and instead go to Eisenhower, who used it as a springboard to the White House. The closest Marshall ever came to a negative comment was to say to close colleagues that, of course, "[A]ny soldier would prefer a field command."

And although Roosevelt was all too prophetic in his prediction of history's treatment of George Marshall—sixty years later most choolchildren haven't the slightest idea who Marshall was and how much he meant to America—the true measure of the man was captured when, reflecting later on the fateful decision, Marshall said, "The issue was simply too great for any personal feeling to be involved."

The short statement succinctly and accurately captures Marshall's true selflessness. George Marshall never considered the personal implications when he weighed a decision or took an action. His only purpose was to serve his country and win the war as quickly and efficiently as possible. As Secretary of War Henry Stimson said to Marshall on May 8, 1945—the day Germany surrendered—"No one who is thinking of himself can rise to true heights. You never thought of yourself."

A Way of Life

In the fall of 1897, George Marshall, then a slender, sixteen-year-old with an "appalling Pittsburgh twang," was late in arriving for the start of his first year at the Virginia Military Institute (VMI) because he was still recovering from a serious case of typhoid.

VMI, which was—and still is—steeped in southern and military tradition, was hard on its newest cadets—patronizingly referred to as "rats." Marshall's new status and his northern Pennsylvanian roots quickly earned him the dubious title of "Yankee rat." All "rats" were subjected to a series of arduous chores and tasks, but the Yankee rat more so than others.

One of the more excoriating and humiliating trials was something called "The Bayonet." The task required the unlucky "rat" to squat naked over the sharp, pointed blade of a bayonet and then, using only the lightly applied pressure of his bare buttocks, hold the blade in an upright position until he was permitted to be relieved by the upper classmen from the embarrassing posture. Unaware of Marshall's condition—the typhoid had left him pale and weak—the upperclassman subjected him to the ordeal and then watched in horror when he, after a prolonged period, collapsed and slashed his buttocks, barely avoiding a much more serious injury.

Under the official rules of VMI at the time, hazing of any sort was strictly forbidden. Unofficially, and as long as no one was hurt, such rituals were overlooked with a wink and a nod. Marshall's wound was of such a serious nature, however, that it required a doctor's attention. As the young, pale Yankee rat was stitched up, the upperclassmen, fearing expulsion, were left to wonder if he would report the incident.

To the relief and surprise of all, Marshall explained away his wound and remained silent as to the true cause. From that moment on, in spite of his regional disadvantages, Marshall was accepted by his peers, and by the end of his first year, he had risen to the position of first corporal of cadets. Two years later he was named captain—the highest-ranking position at VMI. The episode offers an early glimpse into Marshall's willingness to subvert his personal interests to those of the institution he had chosen to join.

On November 27, 1945, the day after he retired from the U.S. Army, President Harry Truman asked the weary and exhausted Marshall—he had had only nineteen days of rest in the preceding six years—to go to China to attempt to negotiate a peaceful resolution to the civil war there. In a letter to his goddaughter, Rose Page, Marshall wrote, "I long for my personal freedom . . . [b]ut here I am." The selfless Marshall could not refuse a request from his president and his country.

Five years later, when he was again called out of retirement to serve as secretary of defense, he explained his decision to his goddaughter this way: "When the president comes down and sits under our oaks and tells me of his difficulties, he has me at a disadvantage." Marshall was at a disadvantage, of course, because his devotion to duty trumped his own personal interests. The president was his Commander-in-Chief, and retired or not, if he was called upon to serve, he would.

But perhaps the most telling example of Marshall's selflessness—or at least what motivated it—occurred later in his life when, after serving as chief of staff of the army (where he earned an annual salary of $10,000) and secretary of state (where he earned $15,000), he repeatedly turned down offers of $1 million or more to write his memoirs. When asked why, Marshall said that the opportunity to serve his country was all the reward he required. In short, his personal interests had been served because the needs of the institutions he served had been met.

Selflessness as a Guide to Action

Marshall's selflessness is not to be confused with a lack of ambition. From the time he served with General John J. Pershing during World War I (and perhaps well before that), Marshall aspired to be army chief of staff—the army's highest-ranking officer. His road was long and hard, but because his personal interests usually mirrored those of the army and the nation, he was able to steadily—but slowly—advance. This was not, however, always the case. Sometimes his selflessness required that he make decisions or take actions that could have been harmful to his prospects for personal advancement. The story of how he stood up to William Howard Taft (the former president) and other powerful individuals in 1916, as they were trying to use their influence to get their friends into the officer corps, as was told in Chapter 1, is one such example. But in early 1941, he faced a similar backlash when he cleared the "dead wood" from the senior ranks of the army and National Guard officer corps.

After helping secure the passage of a law that allowed him to retire hundreds of senior officers, Marshall set about exercising his newly gained authority with ruthless efficiency. Almost instantly, his actions were met with fierce resistance from the aggrieved officers, their wives, as well as supportive politicians and even prominent editorial boards. Marshall refused to back down because he believed that it was the right thing to do. He even offered President Roosevelt his resignation (he still had two full years to go in his tenure) as a sign that he was willing to make the same sacrifice that he was asking of the others. Luckily for the nation, Roosevelt laughed off the suggestion and kept Marshall in his position. As the late Eric Severeid once commented, Marshall's "selfless devotion to duty [was] beyond all influences of public pressure or personal friendship."

Another example of how Marshall's selflessness guided his actions occurred in early 1942 in an encounter with General Hugh Drum. With America now at war, Marshall had the task of assigning generals to various theaters of war around the world. Drum was asked by Secretary of War Stimson to serve in China. Drum—whom Marshall had edged out for the chief of staff position in 1939 (ironically because Roosevelt disliked Drum's penchant for self-promotion, since he often used the national media to portray himself in a flattering light and persuaded influential political allies to lobby for his selection)—deferred, fearing he "would be lost in a minor effort of little decisive consequence." When Marshall learned of Drum's response, he was outraged that a senior officer, in a time of war, would oppose the request of his civilian superior. He called Drum into his office for a heated discussion. Drum sealed his fate by telling Marshall that he felt he "would be more valuable to the country . . . with a mission involving larger responsibilities." (Most likely, he was eyeing the highly coveted position in the European theater). Marshall knew that Drum was more concerned with his personal well-being than the nation's, and he pulled his name from consideration.

Even after Drum reconsidered his decision and begged to be sent to China, Marshall refused, feeling that the selfishness he had displayed earlier was a serious character flaw, which would likely manifest itself in ways detrimental to the interest of the army, its soldiers, and the nation as a whole.

If Marshall could be harsh on those he considered selfish, he could be equally magnanimous with those who he considered to be selfless. After he became president, Dwight Eisenhower recounted an insightful story on this characteristic. Early during the war, Marshall told his staff that "the men that are promoted in this war are going to be the people that are in command," adding that "the staff isn't going to get promoted at all." Turning to Eisenhower, Marshall said, "Now you are a case. I happen to know General [Kenyon] Joyce tried to get you as a division commander . . . [w]ell, that's too bad. You are a brigadier, and you are going to stay a brigadier." Marshall then carried on for a few more minutes before Eisenhower finally spoke up. "I don't give a damn about your promotion and your power to promote to me," Eisenhower said. "You brought me in here for a job . . . [and] I'm going to do my duty." As he left the room, Eisenhower turned around and noticed a slight smile had crossed Marshall's face. Eisenhower was promoted to a command position shortly thereafter—likely because he had passed one of Marshall's most critical tests.[2]

Marshall's preference for such selflessness was by no means limited to general officers. Eisenhower once came upon a forty-year-old man with "distinguished family connections" who was quietly serving in a lowly position. Upon accidentally discovering the situation, Marshall took the unusual action of asking that the man's status be improved for the sole reason that he *didn't* ask for any favor for himself.

Rising Above the Pettiness

Marshall's ability to rise above pettiness constitutes another often-overlooked component of his selflessness. Because he was always focused on the needs of the institutions rather than his own interests, Marshall wasted precious little energy worrying about the little slights that so often divert lesser men.

Most of the biographies written about Marshall cite a conflict between Marshall and General Douglas MacArthur stemming from an incident in World War I in which Pershing's staff supposedly denied MacArthur an opportunity for further battlefield glory. Marshall always downplayed such reports and called it "damned nonsense." However, Marshall's second wife, in a book written after World War II, claimed that "George was the one man MacArthur feared," and she cited this fear as the reason why MacArthur—when he was chief of staff of the army in the early 1930s—ordered Marshall to leave his command post (and a sure path to promotion) to instead serve with the Illinois National Guard in 1933. (MacArthur's action was supposedly designed to keep Marshall from receiving his first star, and therefore keep him out of the running for the chief of staff position in 1935—a position MacArthur wanted to retain for himself.)

Marshall could easily have ascribed ulterior motives, real or perceived, to MacArthur's action and chosen to respond in kind when he became the army's top officer in 1939. Instead, Marshall—who truly admired MacArthur's battlefield leadership skills—consistently acted toward him in a way that demonstrated he only had the nation's best interest at heart. For instance, it was Marshall who urged Roosevelt to recall MacArthur to active duty in 1940 and grant him his old rank (the equivalent of Marshall's own four-star rank). And when MacArthur had to retreat from the Philippines during the early months of war in 1942, it was Marshall, recognizing that the nation was desperately in need of a hero, who personally wrote the citation for MacArthur's Medal of Honor (the country's most distinguished military decoration.) In so doing, he clearly placed the needs of the nation over any past personal slights.

After the war, Marshall continued to demonstrate his ability to rise above personal attacks, even when they were anything but petty. At the height of Joseph McCarthy's witch-hunt for communists, the senator took to the Senate floor and unleashed a vicious 60,000-word diatribe in which he portrayed Marshall as a dupe for communist forces. Later, when Marshall was besieged by friendly and supportive reporters offering him a chance to refute the charges, the always-dignified Marshall responded simply by saying, "I do appreciate that, but if I have to explain at this point that I am not a traitor to the United States, I hardly think it's worth it."

And when Senator William Jenner declared during Marshall's confirmation hearings for secretary of defense that Marshall was "eager to play the role of front man for traitors," President Truman was livid and told Marshall that he was going to "skin [Jenner] alive." Marshall politely redirected the president's energies by saying that it was unnecessary and wryly added, "The stench from that sort of animal is difficult to wash off."

Marshall, better than most people of the time, placed his faith in the ability of the American people to distinguish the truth in the end. By letting his selfless actions speak for themselves, his stature only grew in the years ahead, while McCarthy and his ilk rightfully earned their place in the ignominious ash heap of history.

Dwight Eisenhower—who, shamefully, did not publicly condemn McCarthy's attacks against his old mentor when he was running for president in 1952—later realized the errors of his way and said Marshall was "one of the patriots of this country. Anyone who has lived with him, has worked for him as I have, knows that he is a man of real selflessness."

It is, however, another small story—the kind that often gets easily overlooked—that provides perhaps the most telling example of his selflessness. In late 1951, well after he had gained worldwide fame for his leadership as chief of staff of the army and secretary of state, Marshall was called back to serve as secretary of defense. In terms of protocol, the position placed him behind Secretary of State Dean Acheson—his former deputy. Acheson was aghast at the prospect of Marshall—a man he revered—deferring to him in diplomatic situations. Marshall, however, demanded that protocol be followed. If Acheson entered a room, Marshall followed behind. If Acheson sat at a table, Marshall sat to his right, and if a photo was to be taken, Marshall always stood behind the secretary and slightly off-center.

It was entirely in keeping with his character because Marshall never imagined that his power emanated from himself. Rather, his power came from the institutions he had the privilege of serving, and he never used that power to serve his own needs—he deployed it only for the benefit of his country.

Without a Single "I"

Throughout the war, Marshall consistently refused all citations and military decorations because he felt such awards should only be given to those who won distinction in the combat zones. To do otherwise, he reasoned, would take attention away from those most deserving, harm morale, and thus hurt the very cause to which he had committed himself.

Marshall's selflessness also manifested itself when supporters in Congress attempted to give him his fifth star (the military's highest rank). Marshall—who in no way solicited the promotion—privately argued against the idea because he "didn't want to be beholden to Congress for any rank or anything of that kind. I wanted to be able to go in there with my shirts clean and with no personal ambitions concerned in any way," adding that it was unnecessary because "I could get all I wanted with the rank I had." Marshall further argued against the promotion in deference to his former boss and personal hero, General Pershing, whom he believed had rightly earned the prestigious five-star rank in the First World War.

Only after President Roosevelt—with General Pershing's concurrence—announced his intention to support the proposal did Marshall reluctantly agree to accept a fifth star—and then only on two conditions: One, that his fellow army officers (Eisenhower, MacArthur, and Henry "Hap" Arnold) also receive a fifth star; and, two, that his title be amended to "General of the Army," thus allowing General Pershing to retain the higher title of "General of the Armies."

Marshall's unfailing selflessness was, however, best captured in *Time* magazine's write-up of him in its 1943 Man of the Year issue. In singing his many praises, *Time* wrote that his report to the nation on the progress of the war—which was drafted largely by Marshall himself—was written "without a single 'I'."

Lessons: In His Own Words

"As soon as an ulterior purpose or motive creeps in, then the trouble starts and will gather momentum like a snowball." In 1944 and

1948, George Marshall was among the most popular and esteemed men in America, and his name was constantly brought up as a possible presidential candidate. Given Roosevelt's poor health in 1944 and Truman's perceived unpopularity in 1948, it is not difficult to envision a Marshall candidacy quickly taking hold in a country that desperately needed mature leadership. Yet he consistently and forcefully declined every invitation and opportunity to join the race, saying only that "[p]utting such an idea into a man's head is the first step toward destroying his usefulness." As a result of Marshall's selflessness, Congress (particularly Republicans, who might otherwise have feared his political ambitions) granted him far greater leeway during both his years as chief of staff and secretary of state because they were confident that in supporting his proposals and recommendations, they weren't creating a future presidential candidate.

A number of modern executives and CEOs similarly avoid the limelight and direct all of their considerable talents into growing their businesses. And, as in Marshall's case, it is often their own selflessness that keeps their names from being household names. Jim Collins, in his excellent book *Good to Great: Why Some Companies Make the Leap . . . and Others Don't*, identifies eleven "Level 5 Leaders"—CEOs—whom he defines as individuals who "channel needs away from themselves and into the larger goal of building a great company." Among the people Collins places in this rarified category are George Cain (Abbott Laboratories), Alan Wurtzel (Circuit City), David Maxwell (Fannie Mae), Colman Mockler (Gilette), Darwin Smith (Kimberly Clark), Jim Herring (Kroger), Lyle Everingham (Kroger), Joe Cullman (Philip Morris), Fred Allen

(Pitney Bowes), Cork Walgreen (Walgreens), and Carl Reichardt (Wells Fargo).[3]

Like Marshall, who grew the U.S. Army from a small, continental force of 175,000 into the most powerful army in the world in just six years, these CEOs also presided over the extraordinary growth of their companies. For instance, Darwin Smith, CEO of Kimberly-Clark, generated stock returns four times greater than the general market during his twenty-five-year tenure (and outperformed the like of GE's Jack Welch and Coca-Cola's Roberto Goizueta). Dick Cooley, former CEO of Wells Fargo, outperformed the market by three times during the time he held the helm of his company—during a period in which the banking industry as a whole was outperformed by the market by 62 percent.

Why were they successful? In part, it was talent. In part, it was because these leaders directed all of their considerable talent, time, and energy into growing their organization instead of finding ways to trumpet themselves.

"I attended strictly to business." In 1939, George Marshall was chosen over General Hugh Drum as chief of staff of the army in part because he didn't engage in self-promotion. In fact, Marshall religiously avoided self-promotion, and he even argued that his refusal to engage in it was his strongest asset. To a friendly reporter who was hoping to help Marshall promote his candidacy with a favorable article, Marshall once replied, "My strength within the army has rested on the well-known fact that I attended strictly to business and enlisted no influence of any sort at any time."

Collins argues in his book that when recruiting a new CEO, today's boards of directors would be far better served by looking for the qualities associated with selflessness than concentrating on "the need to hire larger-than-life, egocentric leaders." Collins's research suggests that such leaders, in addition to being better team players, tend to be better lifelong learners and are more willing to listen to, accept, and act on constructive criticism.

Donald Trump once said, "I only do a deal if I think it has the greatest glamour."[4] His comment is not dissimilar to Hugh Drum's quip that his talents would be "lost in a minor effort of little decisive consequence." Good leaders know that "glamour" has little relation to long-term success and that what might look like a minor effort today can quickly turn into a grand opportunity in the future.

The leader who is willing to look beyond his or her own personal benefit and instead toward the long-term interests of the organization is the one who is going to best serve the organization.

"[It] would not appear at all well . . ." Marshall consistently refused personal awards and citations—especially when the nation was at war. The reason is because, as the army's top officer, he wanted to make sure attention was directed at the men and women who were serving in the field. A modern business parallel can be found in the actions of Brad Anderson, CEO of Best Buy Co., Inc. In the spring of 2004, he gave up 200,000 options of Best Buy stock (valued at $7.5 million) and ordered it to instead be given to nonexecutive employees who provided premium service to Best Buy's customers. His action sent an

important message to both workers and investors that he understood he was not the only person who contributed to the success of the organization.

Max De Pree, the former CEO of furniture maker Herman Miller, capped his salary at twenty times that of an hourly worker, saying that leaders who "indulge themselves with lavish perks and trappings of power . . . damage their standing as leaders."[5] Arnold Schwarzenegger did much the same thing when he stated that he would forgo his annual salary while serving as governor of California. Most everyone knows that he is a multimillionaire and doesn't need the money, but his act still sends a strong and symbolic message and enhances his standing as a leader.

"[H]ave no fears regarding my personal reactions . . . act in the best interest of the country." In retrospective, Marshall's refusal to "lift a single finger" on his own behalf when asked by the president if he wanted the European command was an extraordinary act. Marshall understood—just like Roosevelt—that his refusal would deprive him a great place in American history. Yet, he still chose to act in the country's best interest.

In the late 1980s, Len Roberts (now CEO of Radio Shack) accepted the job as CEO of Shoney's (a fast-food restaurant). He knew the company was in debt when he took the position, but he didn't know it was in the midst of a large discrimination case. After reviewing the case, Roberts recommended the company do the right thing and settle the case. The chairman of the company agreed—on the condition that Roberts resign. Even though he played no role in the past discrimination, Roberts agreed because he felt paying the settlement was the morally right thing to do and because it was in the best interest of the company—and not himself.[6]

A more recent example of such selflessness comes from the world of polar exploration. In 2001, Ann Bancroft and Liv Arnesen set out to cross the entire continent of Antarctica. For over three months, they relentlessly drove across the continent in the face of incredible odds. With only 400 miles to go, however, the end of the summer season brought forth severe blizzard conditions. Three years of planning, preparation, and hard work—as well as the glory of the accomplishment—hung in the balance. As they pondered whether they could make it across the final stretch in the little time remaining, Bancroft and Arnesen realized their desire to pursue their own personal goals would jeopardize the lives of the air and ship crews who were waiting to pick them up. With great remorse, they abandoned their dreams. It was a difficult thing to do, but it was the selfless thing to do.[7]

"No, gentlemen, you don't take a post of this sort and then resign when the man who has the constitutional responsibility to make decisions makes one you don't like." In the fall of 1948, President Truman, facing a tough reelection bid, was grappling over the question of recognizing statehood for Israel. In a contentious White House meeting, Clark Clifford, then a young aide to Truman, argued forcefully in its favor. George Marshall, then secretary of state, citing America's strategic reliance on Arab oil, opposed it. After listening to both sides, Truman ruled in favor of recognition. Many members of the cabinet and the White House feared Marshall would resign in protest. To their surprise, he did not. Marshall

understood that he was not the person charged with making the decision. The decision rightly rested with the president.

A similar example from modern history can be found in Secretary of State Colin Powell's prewar advice on the issue of Iraq. In Bob Woodward's book *Plan of Attack*, it is relatively clear that Powell preferred a more methodical approach to going to war with Iraq—one that brought along a greater number of allied partners. When the president selected his more aggressive path, Powell accepted the decision because he understood it was the president's—and not his—decision to make. Moreover, once the decision was made, Powell realized that it was in the nation's best interest that he remain in his position where he could continue to serve his country in trying times.

The Way to Go

Six days after the D-Day invasion, George Marshall traveled to Europe to visit his troops and inspect the massive army that he had, as Churchill said, "called into being." During a private moment with Dwight Eisenhower, Marshall asked his protégé a candid question: "Eisenhower, you've chosen all these commanders or accepted those we sent from Washington. What's the principal quality you look for?" Without a moment of hesitation, Eisenhower responded, "Selflessness." Upon reflection, Eisenhower later admitted that Marshall "himself gave me that idea."[8]

An equally telling incident occurred in 1953 when Eisenhower (who was then president) asked Marshall to travel to England to serve as America's representative at the coronation of Queen Elizabeth II. As he walked down the aisle of Westminster Abbey with General Omar Bradley at his side, Marshall was surprised to see row after row of famous and prominent people rise to their feet. He turned around to see who they were standing for and seeing no one whispered to Bradley, "Who are they rising for?" To which Bradley responded, "You."[9]

After a lifetime of service to the army, his country, and the world, Marshall's selflessness was being recognized. The leaders of the free world were standing in his honor because they knew he always served the greater good.

F O U R

SPEAKING YOUR MIND
The Principle of Candor

He stood right up to the president.
—Secretary of Treasury Henry Morgenthau, writing in his diary of a critical
encounter Marshall had with President Franklin D. Roosevelt

*I mean exactly what I say, and there is no use trying to read between
the lines because there is nothing there to read.*
—George C. Marshall

★ ★ ★ ★ ★

On November 14, 1938, George Marshall, only recently appointed deputy chief of staff of the army, was called to attend his first meeting with President Roosevelt. After three and a half decades, he was finally within reach of his lifelong ambition—being appointed chief of staff—and he was acutely aware that it was Roosevelt who held the key to his selection. It would have only been natural for Marshall to want to make a favorable first impression upon the president.

Called by Roosevelt to discuss his plans to build 10,000 war planes to strengthen the U.S. Army Air Corps, Marshall was grateful for the meeting because he had become alarmed by America's unwillingness to mobilize for a war that appeared increasingly imminent. Shortly into the meeting, however, Marshall was surprised to learn the president only intended to request enough funding from Congress to build the planes—with no money allocated to maintenance or training. He became even more alarmed when none of the president's other civilian and military advisers questioned the wisdom of this policy. Roosevelt then went around the room and asked each adviser for his professional opinion. Each man, in turn, offered his unqualified support for the plan. Eventually, Roosevelt turned to Marshall and asked, "Don't you think so, George?"

Irritated at the president's use of his first name and what he felt was a "misrepresentation of our intimacy," Marshall—without considering the implications on his future aspirations—coolly responded, "I am sorry, Mr. President, but I don't agree with you at all." Roosevelt gave Marshall "a very startled look" and adjourned the meeting.

Once outside, Henry Morgenthau, then secretary of the treasury, came up to Marshall and said, "Well, it's been nice knowing you." The others, Marshall added, "all bade me goodbye and said my turn in Washington was over."

It was Marshall, and not Roosevelt's closest advisers, who had more accurately sized up the president. Less than six months later, Roosevelt called Marshall back to the White House and informed him of his intention to select him as the next chief of staff of the army. The president obviously felt he had found in Marshall an officer who would provide him with honest advice instead of telling him what he thought he wanted to hear.

Before accepting the position, Marshall reinforced his intention to remain candid by telling Roosevelt that he "wanted the right to say what I think, and it would often be unpleasing." Roosevelt responded with a smile and an affirmative "yes."

Marshall replied, "You said 'yes' pleasantly, but it may be unpleasant." Roosevelt nodded again. It only reconfirmed in his mind that he had the right man for the job.

The story of Marshall's first meeting with President Roosevelt, and his subsequent acceptance of the army's top job only on the condition that he have complete freedom to speak his mind, demonstrate Marshall's fourth leadership principle—the principle of candor.

A History of Candor

Marshall's reply to Roosevelt was hardly the first instance of him speaking frankly to powerful individuals. In fact, it could be argued that Marshall's candor played an instrumental—if not the integral—role in his career.

On October 3, 1917, Marshall, then serving as a major in the First Infantry Division, had a famous encounter on the battlefields of France. During a routine inspection, General John J. Pershing, then head of American Expeditionary Forces, became frustrated with what he thought was a lack of proper training in Marshall's division. Pershing launched into a scathing critique of Marshall's division commander. Marshall, believing his commanding officer, General William Sibert, was being unfairly criticized, jumped to his defense and requested an opportunity to speak.

Pershing ignored the request and turned to walk away. Furious and with his face flushed, Marshall physically placed his hand on Pershing and "practically forced him to talk." Marshall began by saying, "[T]here's something to be said here and I think I should say it because I've been here the longest." He proceeded to deliver an extraordinary lecture and spewed forth a "torrent of facts." Marshall's commanding officer and fellow officers were horrified at the outburst. Pershing, however, after listening to the young officer, conceded Marshall his points and asked that he "appreciate the troubles we have."

Marshall responded by saying, "Yes, I know you do, General, but ours are immediate and every day and have to be solved before night." Figuring he was already "up to [his] neck," Marshall then went on to identify Pershing's own headquarters as the source of many of the very problems that the general had just accused his own commanding officer of being unprepared for. Pershing offered to "look into it." Not satisfied with the meek response, Marshall replied that there was no need to "look into the problem," he said "[because] it's a fact."

When the conversation ended, Marshall's fellow officers were convinced that he would be relieved and were ready to bid him farewell. But Pershing, rather than fire Marshall, appreciated his candor, and when the peak of American combat approached in the summer of 1918, he had him transferred to his staff. Within two years, Marshall was one of Pershing's top aides. Marshall would later say of Pershing—his mentor and personal hero— that "[i]t was one of his great strengths that he could listen to things . . . if you convinced him, that was the end of that." It was a trait he would strive to replicate throughout his career.

Telling Difficult Truths

By the fall of 1939, Marshall, as the newly named army chief of staff, began testifying before Congress in his official capacity. His message that America needed to prepare for war was wildly unpopular. Both Congress and the public felt that America's involvement in the First World War had been a terrible mistake. Moreover, Congress was in no mood to divert precious public resources away from an economy that was still in the throes of a serious depression. Marshall refused to cater to public opinion and warned congressional leaders that America would not have the luxury of preparing for a year or more in the next war. "America must be prepared to stand on her own two feet," he said. His words went unheeded, and Congress proceeded to cut the army's budget by 10 percent.

As 1939 turned into 1940, Marshall persisted in his lonely cause. In a private meeting with key congressional leaders, Marshall rattled off the army's shortages in personnel, weapons, tanks, airplanes, and even mundane supplies such as blankets. After he had nearly exhausted himself, he spoke from the heart. "I feel culpable," he said. "My job as chief of staff is to convince you of our needs, and I have utterly failed."[1] His candor, together with his growing reputation among congressmen for truthfulness, swayed many of the participants. Bernard Baruch, an influential adviser to Roosevelt and a strong proponent of America's rearmament, later said Marshall's straight talk was the "turning point" in the struggle to get America to prepare for war.

Convincing Congress was only half of Marshall's battle. He still had not fully convinced President Roosevelt of everything that was required. Facing a tough election in the fall of 1940 and holding on to a false hope that airpower alone could dissuade Germany from further expansionist operations, Roosevelt was reluctant to get too far out in front of the American public by advocating a larger army.

On May 13, 1940, Marshall went to the White House with a budget proposal for $650 million—enough to fund an army of one and a quarter million soldiers. Roosevelt dismissed the proposal out of hand. Treasury Secretary Henry Morgenthau asked that Marshall be allowed to state his case. The president brushed off the request by saying, "I know exactly what he will say . . . [t]here is no necessity for me to hear him at all."

Much as he had done on the battlefield in France two decades earlier, Marshall felt something had to be said and understood he was the person most qualified to say it. "Mr. President, may I have three minutes?" he asked. Without allowing the president an opportunity to respond, Marshall unleashed a torrent of facts and figures: The German army had 140 divisions, the United States only five; weapons were in short supply and critical new weapon systems were not even in production; and the country's industrial capacity had not yet been shifted to reflect the growing threat. In fact, so chaotic was the situation, said Marshall, that the army and navy couldn't even agree to buy the same type of broom. Long after his three minutes had passed, Marshall concluded by looking at the president and saying, "If you don't do something . . . and do it right away, I don't know what is going to happen to this country."

Roosevelt remained silent, and Marshall left the meeting not knowing whether he had convinced him. He needn't have worried; a few days later, Marshall's candid assessment of the situation, together with recent world events, convinced Roosevelt to approve the request. In fact, he was so persuasive that Roosevelt even added an additional $350 million to the figure.

Marshall knew he had no time to rest on his laurels. By the following month, Germany occupied Paris. In August, the

Luftwaffe began assaulting Great Britain. He realized that the United States needed to do even more. By late summer 1940, he was asking Congress for an additional $4 billion. He told Congress, "We must meet the situation that is facing us." When one senator, in an optimistic mood, suggested that the international situation might take a turn for the better in the months ahead and thus allow the United States to abandon a large part of the buildup, Marshall responded by saying, "Senator, I am sorry... I cannot entertain any such hope." He refused to downplay the truth for reasons of political expediency.

Once again, Congress heeded Marshall's candid assessment of the situation and passed the bill. In so doing, America took a second large step toward mobilization by ensuring that vital resources would be available should America need to go to war.

"The Frankest Possible Basis"

Among George Marshall's myriad of responsibilities during the war was the task of briefing division commanders before their deployment overseas. Paul Ransom, who later achieved the rank of major general, wrote that before his briefing he had expected to hear a typical speech. "Instead," Ransom said, "[Marshall] devoted the entire time to excoriating the type of officer who gives answers he thinks the chief wants to hear rather than the hard facts. He strongly impressed upon us... the importance of an officer having the moral courage to report facts, unpleasant as they be, to the ears of the commander, rather than trying to keep bad news from him."[2]

Upon selecting Dwight D. Eisenhower in 1942 to command the Allied Expeditionary Forces, Marshall demanded that their relationship be on the "frankest possible basis," and he emphasized the point by saying, "When you disagree with my point of view, say so, without an apologetic approach."

In another instance, Marshall and his staff were debating with Winston Churchill and other British leaders on the topic of whether the Allied powers should pursue a policy of unconditional surrender with Germany. Al Wedermeyer, then an officer under Marshall, was so opposed to the idea (he believed it would unnecessarily prolong the war and result in greater bloodshed), that he felt compelled to first qualify his remarks by saying that he meant Marshall no disrespect. "Wedermeyer," Marshall snapped, "don't you ever fail to give me your unequivocal expression of views. You would do me a disservice if you did otherwise."[3] Marshall elaborated on why he was so adamant on this the point when he said, "Unless I hear all the arguments against something, I am not sure whether I've made the right decision."

After the war, as secretary of state and in his first meeting with Dean Acheson, then his deputy, Marshall again stressed the importance of candor when he said, "I shall expect of you the most complete frankness, particularly about myself. I have no feelings except those I reserve for Mrs. Marshall."

The Fruits of Honesty

In 1942, Marshall met with V. M. Molotov, the Soviet Union's minister of foreign affairs, to discuss the issue of securing additional supplies for the Soviet Union in its fight with Germany.

Molotov also used the meeting to bring up the issue of whether the United States should open up a second front against Germany in Western Europe by the end of the year.

"What do you want, the second front or [supplies]?" Marshall asked, "It isn't possible to provide both." Patiently, he waited for Molotov's response. As he did, Marshall asked his interpreter whether Molotov's interpreter had accurately translated his question. The aide responded that he had not. Marshall ordered him to repeat his question to Molotov fully. The Russian interpreter once more abbreviated his query and, again, Marshall demanded his question "be translated and passed fully and exactly to Mr. Molotov." The story is important because Marshall later learned that Molotov appreciated his straightforward style and equated it with honesty.[4] This factor was instrumental in helping the United States and the Soviet Union remain on good terms throughout the Second World War.

In one of his first official meetings as secretary of state, Marshall met with French Premier Paul Ramadier, who was extremely concerned over U.S. plans to allow Germany to rearm. After assuring Ramadier that he understood his concerns (Marshall reminded him that he was a participant in both world wars and was well aware of the pain and suffering that had been inflicted on France by Germany), Marshall stated that America would not do anything to jeopardize France's security. He then concluded his remarks by saying, "I am not a diplomat. I mean exactly what I say, and there is no use trying to read between the lines because there is nothing there to read." Knowing Marshall's reputation for candor and integrity, France agreed to the plan, which significantly contributed to the long-term security of Europe.

The most beneficial application of Marshall's candor, however, occurred in relation to the Marshall Plan. During the
Moscow foreign minister's conference in the spring of 1947,
after exercising almost every diplomatic approach and employing "almost brutal assaults" on Josef Stalin in an effort to get him
to reconsider the Soviet Union's newly adopted confrontational
approach, Marshall realized America had to take the lead in
improving the economic situation in postwar Europe.

Marshall returned to the United States and, in a nationwide
radio address, told his fellow citizens that Europe needed help.
In his straightforward style, he said, "[T]he patient is sinking
while the doctors deliberate," and then in his famous speech
before the 1947 graduates of Harvard, he continued with his
candid approach. "I need not tell you that the world situation is
very serious," he said. "[T]he truth of the matter is that Europe's
requirements for the next three or four years for foreign food
and other essential products—principally from America—are so
much greater than her present ability to pay that she must have
substantial additional help or face economic, social, and political deterioration of a very grave character." The blunt, 1,500-
word speech succinctly laid out both the problem and the
solution—and arguably set the stage for one of the greatest and
most successful foreign-aid programs in the history of the world.

Lessons: In His Own Words

*"I am disappointed in all of you. You haven't disagreed with a single
thing I have done all week."* George Marshall uttered this statement just a week after becoming chief of staff of the U.S. Army.

He understood strong leaders must not only be willing to accept criticism and divergent points of view, they must go out of their way to consistently create an atmosphere conducive to candor. Marshall did more than simply preach this message—he lived it. In his first meeting with Marshall, Colonel Joseph T. McNarney presented him with a plan that he had spent a great deal of time thinking about and preparing. When Marshall quickly glanced at it and made a suggested change, McNarney was livid and, in the heat of the moment, blurted out, "Jesus, man, you can't do that!" Fearing afterward that he would be relegated to the bowels of the War Department as a result of his outburst, McNarney confided his concerns to a fellow officer on Marshall's staff who responded, "Don't worry. He likes for people to speak up." The officer was right, and much as General Pershing had promoted Marshall on the basis of their initial candid encounter, so did Marshall promote McNarney.

Many people in business today pay lip service to the importance of candor, yet are quick to "shoot the messenger" or penalize individuals if they offer assessments that run counter to their own ideas. In his book, *In Search of Excellence*, Tom Peters said that such actions only cause unalignment in an organization.

Warren Bennis was even more succinct when he wrote in *Fast Company* in September of 2004 that "cultures of fear abound." He pointed to the Space Shuttle disasters at NASA, the Abu Ghraib prison scandal within the army, and the *USA Today* plagiarism case as classic examples of institutions that encouraged their people to keep their mouths shut and their heads down. Bennis stressed that the solution was for leaders to make it "psychologically safe" for people to speak up.

Alfred Sloan, the legendary CEO who built General Motors, offered a famous anecdote that bears repeating. Frustrated at his leadership team's unwillingness to rock the boat on an important issue, Sloan replied, "I take it we are all in complete agreement on the decision here. Therefore, I propose we postpone further discussion of the matter until our next meeting to give ourselves time to development disagreement and perhaps gain some understanding of what the decision is all about."[5] Sloan, like George Marshall, knew that it was important—indeed necessary—to create a culture of candor.

Other companies that do the same thing include General Electric, with its renowned organizational practice called "Work-Out," a mandatory, monthly, open-forum meeting between managers and employees where problems, inefficiencies, and ineffective practices can be discussed freely. The U.S. Army has "After Action Reviews," in which officers, regardless of rank, are required to provide their honest feedback of what went right and what went wrong during military operations.

"Whenever I find these fellows who seem to have ability and a certain amount of disagreement with what we are doing, I am always interested in seeing them and getting a firsthand impression." This is a corollary to the previous lesson. In addition to encouraging a "culture of candor," Marshall actively encouraged it by seeking out dissenting views. Once a young major came to him with a proposal to modify a piece of ordinance. The general with responsibility for ordinance was furious that the young officer had persisted in his cause, even after he had been told the weapon system was not going to be changed. Marshall called

both men—the major and the general—into his office and asked each man for his rationale. After hearing both sides, Marshall supported the major.

Bill George, the former CEO of Medtronic, tells the story of once receiving an eleven to one vote by his board of directors in favor of an acquisition. He was intrigued by the lone standout and sought him out. After listening to him, George passed on the deal. As George's example demonstrates, good leaders do more than encourage candor. They seek it out.[6]

"I am sorry, Mr. President, but I don't agree with you at all." George Marshall was never afraid to speak his mind—even to the most powerful of men—as he did in his first meeting with President Roosevelt. A few other instances are equally telling. In 1943, Churchill, as he had so many times before, sought to delay the invasion of Europe by proposing an attack on the island of Rhodes. After listening to his argument, Marshall wheeled on Churchill and, in uncharacteristically harsh language, said, "Not one American soldier is going to die on that goddamned beach." The issue was never raised again.

Another time, while serving as President Harry Truman's personal envoy to China, Marshall was charged with negotiating a workable compromise between Mao Tse-tung's communist forces and Chiang Kai-shek's nationalist forces. He was more sympathetic to the nationalist cause, but he soon became convinced that nationalist forces were squandering resources. Marshall bluntly told a group of Chiang's senior ministers, in terms rarely heard in diplomatic circles, "The [nationalist] army is draining 80 to 90 percent of the budget, and if you think the

U.S. taxpayer is going to step into the vacuum this creates, you can go to hell." He was even more candid with Chiang Kai-shek a bit later. "You have broken agreements, you have gone counter to plans," he said. "People have said you were a modern George Washington, but after these things, they will never say it again."

Obviously not all executives and managers are secure enough in themselves to accept such candor, and even fewer are confident in their own ability to actually promote individuals who demonstrate it. However, the leaders who do so (such as Roosevelt and Churchill) understand they can only confront reality by receiving accurate information and honest assessments from their subordinates.

The Naval Institute's well-respected publication, *Proceedings*, occasionally reprints an article that first appeared in the early 1960s. Upon taking command of a new aircraft-carrier battle group, which had recently returned from a lengthy overseas deployment, the admiral called his new staff (which he inherited from his predecessor) to his wardroom, where he stated his intention to cancel all leave for the ship's crew. He then asked each officer for his opinion. The more senior officers either concurred with his suggestion or, alternatively, responded that they would carry his order out. Only a junior officer volunteered a dissenting view. The lieutenant said that it was an awful idea and that, if implemented, would have a negative effect on the morale of the sailors. The lieutenant's fellow officers, including the captain of the carrier, reprimanded him after they had been dismissed by the admiral.

Soon after, the admiral called the lieutenant back into his office. He thanked the young officer for his candor and said he agreed with his assessment. He then told the lieutenant he had floated his idea—which he knew was a horrible one—because he wanted to know which of his new officers he could rely on for honest advice.

In an interview, Jack Welch, the former CEO of General Electric, once said:

> There's still not enough candor in this company. [By that] I mean facing reality, seeing the world as it is rather than as you wish to see it. We've seen over and over again that businesses facing market downturns, tough competition, and more demanding customers inevitably make forecasts that are much too optimistic . . . [c]andid managers—leaders—don't get paralyzed about the fragility of the organization. They tell the people the truth. That doesn't scare them because they realize their people know the truth anyway.[7]

"When you disagree with my point of view say so, without an apologetic approach." In 1947, General Mark Clark—one of the many talented young officers Marshall promoted to positions of command during the war—was serving as the military governor of Austria after the war. The USSR, having been depleted of many of her resources by Germany during the war, was set on recouping some of her loses by disassembling Austria's industrial capacity and shipping the salvageable parts back to Russia. At the time, many of Marshall's top advisers (he was then secretary of state) were supportive of the Soviet actions.

Clark was shocked at the policy and said, "General Marshall, may I say what I think?" Marshall responded by saying, "We know what you think." Clark replied, "Then let me say it again." He then went on to argue that if the USSR was allowed to proceed with the action it would violate all that America had "been fighting for . . . [and] what thousands of men have died for."

Only because he encouraged and expected such candor did Marshall receive the information necessary to change his mind. In this instance, it may have quite literally saved Austria from being plundered of resources it needed to rebuild its economy.

Dick Brown, former CEO of Electronic Data Systems Corporation (EDS), also expected his managers to practice "intense candor" at all times. In the book *Execution: The Discipline of Getting Things Done*, the authors recount a story when one of Brown's subordinates expressed some anxiety that the company was moving too fast on a particular organizational change. Brown immediately seized the question and turned it around on all of his managers. He said, "I would like anyone . . . who is worried about where we are going and worried about the fact that we will probably fail, [to] tell me so right now." He then added, "Don't be afraid to say you are. If you think we're making a big mistake and heading for the reef, speak up now." By emphasizing a policy of "truth over harmony," Brown has continually avoided problems by encouraging "intense candor."[8] Another person who employed a similar philosophy was Horace B. Deets, the former executive director of AARP. One of the reasons he was able to grow the organization into one of the most influential lobbying organizations in America is because he embraced dissent and "encourage[d] as much openness and contrary views as possible."[9]

"Senator, I am sorry that I cannot entertain any such hope." In the summer of 1940, when George Marshall uttered this sentence, he could perhaps have been forgiven if, as a way to secure the senator's vote, he had simply concurred with the senator's wishful thinking that the war in Europe could be avoided. Such an act, while politically expedient in the short run, would have begun to subtly erode Marshall's credibility with Congress. Furthermore, it would have held out the hope of a false promise where none actually existed.

Bill George displayed similar candor when he told Medtronic shareholders that they did not "come first"—as so many CEOs like to tell their shareholders. In fact, he had the courage to tell them they actually came third, behind Medtronic's customers and employees. George expected to receive a lot of negative reaction from shareholders, but it never came because the shareholders recognized the truth behind his statement. If the company—and its shareholders—were truly interested in achieving long-term gains, their interests had to be secondary to the customers and employees.

Ronald Drapeau, Callaway Golf Company's former CEO, was known to be refreshingly candid about both the good news as well as the bad news at his company. He took special care to explain the reasons for any poor performance, and he candidly identified the weaknesses that contributed to the poor performance, afterward outlining the corrective action that was being taken.

Like Marshall, executives such as George and Drapeau understand that people not only accept the truth if it is explained to them candidly, they actually appreciate it.

"I am not a diplomat. I mean exactly what I say and there is no use trying to read between the lines because there is nothing to read there." George Marshall never minced his words. As he once told long-time Abilene, Kansas, resident Dwight D. Eisenhower when he was first preparing to deal with the Russians, "Approach them in simple Main Street Abilene style." Marshall knew from experience that the Soviets appreciated candor and associated it with honesty.

The Russians are not alone in that assessment. Most people associate straight talk with honesty, which is why it is so surprising that many of today's CEOs continue to hide behind the veneer of institutional "corporate speak" in an attempt to mask uncomfortable facts. Some leaders, like Anne Mulcahy, the CEO of Xerox Corporation, refuse to play the game. And on occasion, such candor can be painful. For example, Mulcahy once declared Xerox's business model "unsustainable," and the company's stock plummeted 26 percent in a single day. Her frankness, over time, however, has not only helped her company recover from that initial setback, it has also helped employees deal with the significant amount of change she has implemented, while also earning her the respect of investors, analysts, employees, and customers.

The Way to Go

After his speech at Harvard in which he outlined the rationale for the Marshall Plan, Marshall was acutely aware that tangible action was needed to translate the idea into an effective program. Thus, with the same vigor that he demonstrated in getting America to

1900-1901. Lexington, Virginia. Cadets holding commissioned rank at Virginia Military Institute. Marshall, First Captain and Commander of Company A, is third from left in the front row. *Courtesy of the George C. Marshall Research Library, Lexington, Virginia. GCMRL# 878.*

Ca. 1908. Fort Leavenworth, Kansas. (*left*) As Second Lieutenant, before his graduation from Staff College, and (*right*) First Lieutenant George C. Marshall. *Courtesy of the George C. Marshall Research Library, Lexington, Virginia. GCMRL#s 98 and 1505.*

World War I. On the Western Front. Marshall served as chief aide to General John J. Pershing, Commander in Chief of the American Expeditionary Force. *Courtesy of the George C. Marshall Research Library, Lexington, Virginia. GCMRL# 129.*

1930-1931. Fort Benning, Georgia. Assistant Commandant George C. Marshall with department heads and instructors at the Infantry School where he taught. Front row, left to right: Lieutenant Colonel Morrison C. Stayer, Lieutenant Colonel Joseph W. Stilwell, Lieutenant Colonel Marshall, Major William F. Freehof, Major Edwin F. Harding. Back row: Captain Howard J. Liston, Major Omar N. Bradley, Major Emil W. Leard, First Lieutenant Fremont B. Hodson. *Courtesy of the George C. Marshall Research Library, Lexington, Virginia. GCMRL# 1086.*

1900-1901. Lexington, Virginia. Cadets holding commissioned rank at Virginia Military Institute. Marshall, First Captain and Commander of Company A, is third from left in the front row. *Courtesy of the George C. Marshall Research Library, Lexington, Virginia. GCMRL# 878.*

Ca. 1908. Fort Leavenworth, Kansas. (*left*) As Second Lieutenant, before his graduation from Staff College, and (*right*) First Lieutenant George C. Marshall. *Courtesy of the George C. Marshall Research Library, Lexington, Virginia. GCMRL#s 98 and 1505.*

World War I. On the Western Front. Marshall served as chief aide to General John J. Pershing, Commander in Chief of the American Expeditionary Force. *Courtesy of the George C. Marshall Research Library, Lexington, Virginia. GCMRL# 129.*

1930-1931. Fort Benning, Georgia. Assistant Commandant George C. Marshall with department heads and instructors at the Infantry School where he taught. Front row, left to right: Lieutenant Colonel Morrison C. Stayer, Lieutenant Colonel Joseph W. Stilwell, Lieutenant Colonel Marshall, Major William F. Freehof, Major Edwin F. Harding. Back row: Captain Howard J. Liston, Major Omar N. Bradley, Major Emil W. Leard, First Lieutenant Fremont B. Hodson. *Courtesy of the George C. Marshall Research Library, Lexington, Virginia. GCMRL# 1086.*

September 1, 1939. Secretary of War Harry H. Woodring looks on as Major General Emory S. Adams, Adjutant General of the War Department, swears in George Marshall as Chief of Staff of the United States Army. *Courtesy of the George C. Marshall Research Library, Lexington, Virginia. GCMRL# 970.*

August 1941. Placentia Bay. Franklin Roosevelt and Winston Churchill with Marshall and Admirals Ernest King and Harold Stark. *Courtesy of the George C. Marshall Research Library, Lexington, Virginia. GCMRL# 1655.*

1941. Fort Myer, Virginia. Marshall on an early morning ride with his dog, Fleet. *Courtesy of the George C. Marshall Research Library, Lexington, Virginia. GCMRL# 16.*

July 1944. National Airport, Washington, D.C. Marshall greets Free French leader General Charles deGaulle, after the invasion of France. *Courtesy of the George C. Marshall Research Library, Lexington, Virginia. GCMRL# 7127.*

September 1, 1939. Secretary of War Harry H. Woodring looks on as Major General Emory S. Adams, Adjutant General of the War Department, swears in George Marshall as Chief of Staff of the United States Army. *Courtesy of the George C. Marshall Research Library, Lexington, Virginia. GCMRL# 970.*

August 1941. Placentia Bay. Franklin Roosevelt and Winston Churchill with Marshall and Admirals Ernest King and Harold Stark. *Courtesy of the George C. Marshall Research Library, Lexington, Virginia. GCMRL# 1655.*

1941. Fort Myer, Virginia. Marshall on an early morning ride with his dog, Fleet. *Courtesy of the George C. Marshall Research Library, Lexington, Virginia. GCMRL# 16.*

July 1944. National Airport, Washington, D.C. Marshall greets Free French leader General Charles deGaulle, after the invasion of France. *Courtesy of the George C. Marshall Research Library, Lexington, Virginia. GCMRL# 7127.*

October 6, 1944. Orly Airport, Paris. Inspection trip. Marshall with Secretary of State James Byrnes; Supreme Commander Dwight D. Eisenhower (*left*); and commander of the Twelfth Army, Omar N. Bradley (*right*). Having noted their leadership promise as young officers in the thirties, Marshall, at this point, could rest assured that his decision to move Eisenhower and Bradley up the chain of command was a sound one. *Courtesy of the George C. Marshall Research Library, Lexington, Virginia. GCMRL# 3201A.*

March 1946. China. Marshall seen here in discussion with Mao Tse-tung. *Courtesy of the George C. Marshall Research Library, Lexington, Virginia. GCMRL# 2505.*

June 5, 1947. Cambridge, Massachusetts. Honorary degree recipients at Harvard's commencement exercises. Front row, left to right: J. Robert Oppenheimer, University of Chicago President Ernest Colwell, George C. Marshall, President James Bryant Conant, General Omar N. Bradley, T. S. Eliot, and Senator James W. Wadsworth. Back row, left to right: W. A. Dwiggins, Professor George H. Chase, W. Hodding Carter, I. A. Richards, William F. Gibbs, and Frank L. Boyden. *Courtesy of the George C. Marshall Research Library, Lexington, Virginia. GCMRL# 7143.*

(*left*) 1949. Marshall as United States Secretary of State. *Courtesy of the George C. Marshall Research Library, Lexington, Virginia. GCMRL# 719.* (*right*) September 1951. General and Mrs. Marshall at home in their garden. *Courtesy of the George C. Marshall Research Library, Lexington, Virginia. GCMRL# 291.*

October 6, 1944. Orly Airport, Paris. Inspection trip. Marshall with Secretary of State James Byrnes; Supreme Commander Dwight D. Eisenhower (*left*); and commander of the Twelfth Army, Omar N. Bradley (*right*). Having noted their leadership promise as young officers in the thirties, Marshall, at this point, could rest assured that his decision to move Eisenhower and Bradley up the chain of command was a sound one. *Courtesy of the George C. Marshall Research Library, Lexington, Virginia. GCMRL# 3201A.*

March 1946. China. Marshall seen here in discussion with Mao Tse-tung. *Courtesy of the George C. Marshall Research Library, Lexington, Virginia. GCMRL# 2505.*

June 5, 1947. Cambridge, Massachusetts. Honorary degree recipients at Harvard's commencement exercises. Front row, left to right: J. Robert Oppenheimer, University of Chicago President Ernest Colwell, George C. Marshall, President James Bryant Conant, General Omar N. Bradley, T. S. Eliot, and Senator James W. Wadsworth. Back row, left to right: W. A. Dwiggins, Professor George H. Chase, W. Hodding Carter, I. A. Richards, William F. Gibbs, and Frank L. Boyden. *Courtesy of the George C. Marshall Research Library, Lexington, Virginia. GCMRL# 7143.*

(*left*) 1949. Marshall as United States Secretary of State. *Courtesy of the George C. Marshall Research Library, Lexington, Virginia. GCMRL# 719.* (*right*) September 1951. General and Mrs. Marshall at home in their garden. *Courtesy of the George C. Marshall Research Library, Lexington, Virginia. GCMRL# 291.*

February 28, 1950. Marshall, as President of the American Red Cross, pins a Red Cross button on the lapel of President Truman prior to Truman's White House address asking Americans to respond to the "Great American Appeal" for dollars to aid the unfortunate. *Courtesy of the George C. Marshall Research Library, Lexington, Virginia. GCMRL# 3019.*

November 15, 1950. The Pentagon, Washington, D.C. Secretary of Defense Marshall and Deputy Secretary Robert A. Lovett witness the swearing in of Mrs. Anna H. Rosenberg as Assistant Secretary of Defense. Felix Larkin (*left*), the department's general counsel, administers the oath. *Courtesy of the George C. Marshall Research Library, Lexington, Virginia. GCMRL# 789.*

October 16, 1959. A cartoon by wartime cartoonist Bill Mauldin commemorates the life of General Marshall. The two GIs, created by Mauldin during World War II to convey how events during the war affected civilian soldiers drafted for Army service overseas, react to news of Marshall's death. *Courtesy of the George C. Marshall Research Library, Lexington, Virginia. GCMRL# 36.*

February 28, 1950. Marshall, as President of the American Red Cross, pins a Red Cross button on the lapel of President Truman prior to Truman's White House address asking Americans to respond to the "Great American Appeal" for dollars to aid the unfortunate. *Courtesy of the George C. Marshall Research Library, Lexington, Virginia. GCMRL# 3019.*

November 15, 1950. The Pentagon, Washington, D.C. Secretary of Defense Marshall and Deputy Secretary Robert A. Lovett witness the swearing in of Mrs. Anna H. Rosenberg as Assistant Secretary of Defense. Felix Larkin (*left*), the department's general counsel, administers the oath. *Courtesy of the George C. Marshall Research Library, Lexington, Virginia. GCMRL# 789.*

MAULDIN

October 16, 1959. A cartoon by wartime cartoonist Bill Mauldin commemorates the life of General Marshall. The two GIs, created by Mauldin during World War II to convey how events during the war affected civilian soldiers drafted for Army service overseas, react to news of Marshall's death. *Courtesy of the George C. Marshall Research Library, Lexington, Virginia. GCMRL# 36.*

prepare before entering World War II, Marshall began selling his idea to Congress. As always, Marshall did not balk from telling people the difficult truths. "This program," he said, "will cost our country billions of dollars. It will impose a burden on the American taxpayer. It will require sacrifices today in order that we may enjoy security and peace tomorrow." Then, without flinching or apologizing, he informed Congress that the price tag for the program would be between $15 billion and $17 billion.

In an era where America is facing comparable threats from terrorists who seek to undermine our way of life, it is still hard to find leaders willing to forthrightly tell the public that the menacing challenge may "impose a burden on the taxpayer." Instead, a great many politicians feel compelled to go in the opposite direction and promise the public "gain without pain," or tell them they are "entitled" to tax cuts, cheap prescription drugs, and an endless number of questionable public subsidies and programs at the same time the country is waging war.

With a number of serious long-term problems confronting America—from the stability of our Social Security and Medicare systems to the very real threat of chemical, biological, and nuclear terrorism—it is all too rare to hear our leaders remind the public that sound policy often requires, as Marshall said, "sacrifices today in order that we may enjoy security and peace tomorrow."

By adhering to Marshall's unbending principle of candor, today's business and political leaders may not always achieve popularity but, chances are, they will find something even rarer—and far more valuable: respect.

F I V E

LAYING THE GROUNDWORK
The Principle of Preparation

The true organizer of victory.
> —Winston Churchill on Marshall's role in the Second World War

Study the first six months of the next war.
> —George C. Marshall's dictum to his students at Fort Benning

★ ★ ★ ★ ★

In the spring of 1917, George Marshall was in the midst of preparing the U.S. Army for the war in Europe when he found time to grant nine newly married second lieutenants a few days of leave. Upon returning from their short honeymoons, the officers all joined Marshall on board the *Tendadores*, the first American troop ship to set sail for France.

As the *Tendadores* eased out of New York Harbor and into the Atlantic Ocean, Marshall was in a gloomy mood. The First American Division had been pulled together from four different infantry regiments, and many of the men were either straight from the backwoods of Kentucky and West Virginia or immigrants with only limited knowledge of the English language. Their "complete ignorance of their weapons or anything," as Marshall later said, only served to darken his mood.

But, as he sat on the deck of the ship, his mood began to brighten as he watched the sailors rig a gun for target practice.

Soon, however, even this proved to be an illusion. "The only thing they succeeded in hitting," said Marshall later, "was the horizon and the foreground." The shoddy performance had a disastrous effect on morale, and Marshall thought to himself, "My God, even the naval part isn't organized, and we are starting off to Europe."

The situation may have been recalled later with a touch of humor had not the effect of America's unpreparedness been so disastrous. It took nearly a full year to train U.S. troops in France before they were ready to fight, and the high casualty rates the Americans suffered were due, in large part, to the soldiers' lack of peacetime training. Of the nine young officers Marshall granted a short honeymoon, eight were killed in action.

"The bitter lesson of unpreparedness," as he called it, never faded from his memory, and the "one great lesson" he drew from his experience in the First World War was that the "unprepared nation is helpless in a great war." The experience played an important role in the development of Marshall's fifth leadership principle—the principle of preparation.

A History of Preparation

In 1910, while on an extended vacation in England, Marshall spent many hours watching and detailing the activities of the British Army. In 1913, again while on vacation, he spent part of his time in Japan studying the battlefields of the 1905 Russo-Japanese War and familiarizing himself with the tactics that contributed to Japan's stunning victory. Marshall was under no obligation to do these things, but they suggest that he lived by the advice he once gave to a junior officer: "Keep your wits about you and your eyes open; keep working hard; sooner or later the opportunity will present itself, and then you must be prepared both tactically and temperamentally to profit by it."

In both instances, his hard work paid off. Less than eight years after his time in Great Britain, Marshall found himself an ally of the British in the First World War. Three decades later, he was engaged in a savage war with Japan, and he was able to apply some of the things he learned during that long-ago vacation.

Marshall's most valuable lesson in the importance of preparation, however, came after his transfer to General John J. Pershing's staff, when he received a firsthand view of the complexities of modern warfare. In his previous positions, he had been charged with the movement of modest numbers of troops and equipment and "struggled with the concrete propositions of feeding, clothing, training, marching, and fighting the men." In his new capacity, his mind was filled with "questions of ocean tonnage, ports of debarkation, and the construction of docks and great depots." Marshall quickly learned that a successful war effort did not depend simply on how the troops and equipment were used at the point of battle; rather, success relied more on mundane issues, such as how resources got to the battlefield and whether they arrived in time and in sufficient number to positively affect the outcome of the battle.

Throughout the war, Marshall itched to get back into a position where he could command troops in battle, but his talent for staff work became so well-regarded that when he applied to return to the battlefield, his commanding officer denied the request because he doubted whether Marshall "had an equal in the army." In fact, Marshall's unique skills actually worked against him. Because he was not allowed to command troops, Marshall missed his opportunity to be promoted to brigadier general and would have to wait an additional eighteen years before he achieved the rank. His commanding officer did, however, recommend that he be promoted to the operations staff of general headquarters.[1]

It was a position that happened to be a blessing in disguise. Marshall was charged with planning and preparing two of the largest American-led offensive operations of the First World War—the Saint Mihiel and the Meuse-Argonne offensives.

Marshall's job was initially complicated by the fact that he had to orchestrate both plans simultaneously. It was a scheme of almost unbelievable complexity that required moving hundreds of thousands of troops. Marshall later claimed it was "the toughest nut I had to crack in France." The Saint Mihiel offensive, which was the easier of the two operations, called for seven American divisions to launch a coordinated attack against an exposed German position. Within two days, the U.S. forces had captured 16,000 German prisoners and gained hold of the position.

The Meuse-Argonne portion of the operation was far more intricate. Eleven French and Italian divisions—consisting of more than 200,000 troops—had to be replaced with 600,000 American troops (400,000 of which would be coming directly from Saint Mihiel). In addition to the troops, 900,000 tons of supplies, 3,000 heavy guns, and thousands of horses and other vehicles had to be moved into place and, in order to maintain the element of surprise, it had to be done in the dark of night.

By all accounts, "Marshall's planning was a logistical feat of unprecedented proportions, and it succeeded brilliantly."[2] The offensive, which was launched on September 26 (two full days ahead of what Ferdinand Foch, France's top general, considered possible), caught the Germans completely by surprise, and it didn't stop until the allies achieved victory on November 11, 1918—Armistice Day.

The Power of Persistence

The satisfaction Marshall felt over the fruits of his preparation and planning quickly faded in the postwar euphoria of America's victory. Upon his return to America in 1919, Marshall watched with frustration as both the American public and Congress forgot "the bitter lesson of unpreparedness." In a speech given in 1923, Marshall documented the steady decline in the size of the army. In the summer of 1919, he noted, the army stood at 846,000; a year later it was reduced to 200,000; and by the time of his speech, it was a shadow of its former self and stood at only 130,000 troops.

Worried that America was on the verge of repeating "our errors of the past," Marshall urged his audience that the solution was to educate and "enlighten" public opinion. He emphasized that the public needed to understand how the failure of the United States to prepare for war was paid for in human lives; the public also needed to know how "narrow the margin of success [was]." He bemoaned the fact that schoolchildren could recite the day America declared war on Germany but only "one in a thousand" knew it was a full year before Americans actually started fighting.

Recognizing that public sentiment was opposed to a sizable army for a variety of reasons, Marshall came to the realization that the key to future preparation lay with a citizen army, saying, "[I]f we fail in the development of a citizen army we will be impotent in the first year of a major war."

After he left his position as aide to General Pershing, Marshall's ability to effect the development of a citizen-based army was limited in nature, but he refused to stop preparing the army for the possibility of a future war. As an instructor at Fort Benning, in addition to completely changing the curriculum (a topic covered in Chapter Six), Marshall was instrumental in helping his students prepare for the faster, more mobile war of the future by making exercises more realistic through the use of live ammunition, airplanes, and tanks. Above all, however, Marshall continuously stressed the need to "study the first six months of the next war."

By 1938, when Marshall returned to Washington, D.C. as chief of the War Plans Division, he immediately took up the issue of preparation. He could not have undertaken his task at a more difficult time in American history. In 1938, isolationism had reached its peak. So fierce was the sentiment that Congress had even passed a constitutional amendment requiring a national referendum before allowing America to enter into any war. (The amendment, which passed by a majority vote of 60 percent, did not advance because it failed to achieve a two-thirds majority, as all constitutional amendments must.) The Depression and the suspicion of any U.S foreign involvement only served to heighten the public's disinterest in building up the military.

Undeterred, Marshall pressed on. In one of his earliest appearances before Congress, he said, "We assume that almost any war of the future will at least start in the air, and that means that we must have available an adequate amount of material and personnel—trained personnel—ready to function the first day of war." Congress politely listened, but refused to heed Marshall's call for preparation. So hostile was the climate in Washington that some congressmen even objected to the money that was being spent on training maneuvers because mistakes were being made. When asked about the errors, Marshall responded, "My God, senator, that's the reason I do it. I want the mistake down in Louisiana [where the army held its largest exercises at the time], not over in Europe, and the only way to do this thing is to try it out, and if it doesn't work, find out what we need to make it work." It was a succinct defense of the importance of preparation, but it got Marshall nowhere.

Only as the world situation continued to worsen did Congress begin to listen more closely to Marshall. But, as he so often did, rather than accept what Congress was willing to provide, Marshall—now chief of staff—pushed them further. "We need to be prepared to meet the worst situation that may develop," he said. Time was so short that Marshall even asked for equipment and supplies for the onslaught of civilians he felt would need to be drafted into the army. Given that Congress had not even authorized the draft yet, it was an extraordinarily presumptuous act.

By mid-1940, after the fall of France, he was granted most of the equipment he requested, and Congress enacted the draft. By the middle of 1941, the international situation had become even more serious, and Marshall realized it was imperative for him—

and the army—to begin thinking in more strategic terms and preparing on a still greater scale.

Up to that point, army planners had primarily been concerned with planning for a continental war. The farthest their international outlook stretched was to the defense of the Western Hemisphere—and the perceived Nazi threat to Latin America. Thus, he ordered a survey of all requirements of the U.S. Army, U.S. Navy, and British forces—which the United States was supplying under the terms of the Lend-Lease Program. He did so, he later said, because he didn't want to make decisions that were either "too haphazard" or that were made "under the emotion of a single moment."

When war finally did come, America was much better prepared than it otherwise would have been because of Marshall's relentless efforts.

"The True Organizer"

Marshall was a firm believer that people fought better if they understood what the war was "all about." To address this issue, he commissioned movies, books, and even newspapers such as the *Stars and Stripes* to help explain the rationale of the war, to share lessons learned from other battles, and to highlight the successes of troops around the world. In one case, Marshall even commissioned a million copies of a booklet entitled *Fighting in Guadalcanal.* He wrote a brief foreword to the book, saying, "Soldiers and officers alike should read these notes and seek to apply lessons. We *must* cash in on the experience which these and other brave men have paid for in blood."

An integral component of Marshall's preparation lay in his deep understanding of the importance of logistics. In 1943, some congressmen and business leaders began to question the size and scope of the army's buildup. Marshall addressed these concerns in a speech to the National Association of Manufacturers. In his talk, he stressed the importance of long-range planning.[3] And although he was aware that some people in his audience thought the army didn't "know what we are doing or where we are going," Marshall assured them that all of the army's actions were taken only after years of study and research. He then went on to criticize many of the army's detractors by saying that too many of their opinions were formed "without knowledge of the logistical requirements" of modern warfare. In fact, Marshall placed so much emphasis on logistics that it once caused his naval counterpart, Admiral Ernest King, to quip, "I don't know what the hell this logistics is that Marshall is always talking about, but I want some of it."[4] A German prisoner near the end of war, however, paid Marshall the ultimate compliment when he said, "I know how you won the war. You piled up all the equipment and let it fall on us." It was a tribute to Marshall's ability to focus on the essential—but unglamorous—aspects of war.[5]

Another component of Marshall's extraordinary talent for preparation was his penchant for immersing himself in the details of every project. This characteristic was vital in giving Marshall his "command presence" when meeting with the president, Congress, or any other important constituencies. He used his knowledge of small details and obscure facts to communicate to audiences of every variety that he grasped—better than anyone else—what needed to be done and why. His command of the facts was so impressive that before the start of a press conference, he could go around the room and ask the reporters what their questions were, then, in the course of his discussion, he would turn to the reporter and answer their particular query. The level of trust and confidence such performances inspired is difficult to measure, but an aide to President Roosevelt once remarked that Marshall inspired confidence and reverence wherever he went.

The measure of the importance of all Marshall's preparation was obviously the effect that it had on the outcome of the war. Without America's material aid it is quite possible that neither Britain nor the Soviet Union would have survived the initial German onslaught. Other experts have argued that if America had not taken the steps Marshall advocated and fought so hard to achieve in the prewar years from 1939–1941, the war might have lasted until 1947, or even 1948, and resulted in hundreds of thousands more casualties.

The effects of Marshall's preparation were, however, best captured by Winston Churchill, when after the war, he wondered aloud:

> It remains a mystery, as yet unexplained, how the very small staffs which the United States kept during the years of peace were able not only to build up the armies, but also to find the leaders. How you should have been able to preserve the art not only of creating mighty armies at the stroke of a wand— but [of] leading and guiding those armies upon a scale incomparably greater than anything that was prepared for or ever dreamed of.

The truth, of course, was that there was no mystery. The answer lay in Marshall's relentless preparation. It was he who mobilized the mighty industrial resources of a reluctant nation. He was the one who trained and selected the officers, and who had the foresight to call into action the citizen-soldiers who won the war. It is for these reasons that Winston Churchill rightly called him "the true organizer of victory."

Lessons: In His Own Words

"We have to be prepared to meet the worst situation that may develop." This was George Marshall's warning to Congress in 1940. It heeded his advice—but just barely. The sad fact is that it is difficult to get organizations, large or small, and even nations to prepare for possible emergencies. Three years after 9/11, an American Management Association survey revealed that 51 percent of businesses still do not have a crisis management plan, and 59 percent do not have a written plan. Jon Goldberg, an executive vice president at PR21 Inc., and a specialist in crisis management, warns, "It's no longer a question of if we face a crisis but when." And much like Marshall, who always stressed the need to "prepare for the unpreparable," Goldberg now reminds his clients that "the most unthinkable scenarios can happen." The basic steps of a crisis management plan are:

1. *Risk Assessment.* Identify all potential crisis scenarios.

2. *Preparation.* Identify external resources that may need to be accessed, and establish policies and procedures for dealing with media and customers.

3. *Monitoring/Alert Systems.* Develop early-warning systems based on a real-time analysis of an organization's information systems.

4. *Simulation/Training.* Conduct drills to simulate real-life situations.

5. *Feedback/Continuous Improvement.* Regularly review risks and vulnerabilities; maintain continuous employee training.

Goldberg, when addressing audiences, now concludes with some advice that Marshall would have appreciated: "An organization can never be too prepared for a crisis, but it can be well prepared."[6]

"Every hour of delay . . . means millions of money." This was George Marshall's message to the Congress of Industrial Organizations in the spring of 1945. He was urging the audience not to get complacent with the Allied victories in Europe. He knew that the best way to end the war quickly in both Europe and Japan—and save lives and money—was to stay prepared. Marshall's skill for preparation, however, was by no means limited to the war. Upon becoming secretary of state in 1947, Marshall officially created the policy planning staff with the State Department and charged it with creating a long-term strategy of enhancing national security. Marshall named George Kennan to head the group, and he responded by developing the basis of the containment strategy, which created the foundation upon which European and American security rested during the Cold War.

The Royal Dutch/Shell Group of Companies continues to do one of the best jobs of any company in preparing for the future.

Since the early 1970s, it has employed a small team called the scenario-planning group. The group develops different scenarios and alternative visions of the future based on technological, demographic, environmental, and geopolitical factors and has accurately and consistently predicted both threats and opportunities well ahead of competitors.[7]

"The tendency already is to relax . . . that's what we have to fight against." This was Marshall's comment after he had helped the U.S. military rebuild itself (for a third time) during the Korean War, when political forces were again clamoring for a reduction in the size of the army. After seeing the cost of unpreparedness in three consecutive wars, Marshall vowed not to let it happen again and, as secretary of defense, he was instrumental in proposing and passing a defense budget that finally allowed the country to maintain a strong military.

Since his selection as CEO of General Electric Company, Jeffrey Immelt has significantly bolstered GE's research and development budget. One reason he has is because he understands that his company cannot relax, in spite of its past success. The exponential advance of knowledge and new, disruptive technologies—technologies that threaten to replace or displace old existing industries—is a very real threat, and one critical way Immelt fights "the tendency to relax" is to invest heavily in new, emerging technologies.

"You have to check on things if you want them done." George Marshall was a stickler for confirming that people had followed through on their assignments and delivered on their promises.

Noel Tichy, in his book *The Leadership Engine*, called Larry Bossidy, the former CEO and chairman of Honeywell, the "master of the follow-up." He documented how Bossidy met with his managers three times a year to review everything from personnel and strategy to reviewing operations. After each meeting, Bossidy would follow up with a letter saying, in effect, "Here is what I liked about your plan. Here is what I didn't like, and here is what we agreed you do about those concerns."[8]

"[K]eep your wits about you and your eyes open; keep working hard. Sooner or later the opportunity will present itself, and then you must be prepared both tactically and temperamentally to profit by it." Marshall once offered this advice to a young officer. It was more than just words; Marshall worked in relative obscurity for thirty-four years before he was promoted to general. But, once promoted, he performed superbly because he used every post and assignment along the way to better prepare himself for the top job.

Anne Mulcahy, the CEO of Xerox Corporation, has been called the "accidental CEO." Before being named CEO, she worked in sales for Xerox for sixteen years and had been the head of its human resources department and chief of staff to the CEO. When she was asked to take the helm, the company had a debt of $17 billion and only $154 million in cash. Still, she accepted the challenge—partly out of loyalty to the company and partly because she knew she was prepared. Her preparation appears to be paying off. Just a few years into her tenure, Xerox has halved its debt, significantly bolstered its cash position, and stabilized its prospects for long-term growth.

"When you don't have the strength, you don't hit a man across the face and call him names." While secretary of state from 1947 to 1949, George Marshall offered this advice to more hawkish elements in America who were advocating that a more aggressive (i.e., militaristic) stance be taken against the Soviet Union in the Cold War. As she had done so many other times before, America had allowed the army to atrophy, and Marshall understood the country was simply not capable of defeating the Soviet Union in a conventional war at the time.

One of the most critical mistakes new businesses—especially new start-ups—make is being too aggressive in their projections. It is critical that the assumptions and projections be realistic. Plans that show market penetration, operating margin, and revenues-per-employee figures that are poorly reasoned, internally inconsistent, or simply unrealistic greatly damage the credibility of the entire business plan and risk losing the backing of financial supporters. In contrast, well-reasoned financial assumptions and projections—while perhaps lacking eye-catching numbers—communicate operational maturity and credibility.

The lesson for business leaders who wish to enter a new field or go head-to-head with an established competitor is that being well prepared is essential. To do anything less not only risks defeat, it risks possible destruction.

"Put it on a single page." George Marshall demanded brevity. He often said that if a problem hadn't been reduced to a single page, it had not been sufficiently thought through.

Today's business world is moving at exponential speed. CEOs, managers, and supervisors are all being overwhelmed with information. One way to deal with the situation is to demand that both written documents and oral presentations be limited in nature.

Betsy Bernard, a former AT&T president, captured this idea when she said that one of her key leadership rules was: "Get to the bloody point." Bernard not only agrees with Marshall's belief that complex issues can be communicated quickly if given advanced thought, she also argues for brevity on the grounds that "time is money" and that people who cannot express themselves quickly are simply wasting other people's time.[9]

Peter Lynch, the well-known mutual fund manager who has encountered many CEOs, has said that if a CEO couldn't tell his company's story in less than two minutes something was wrong—namely, he knew that the CEO had not even done enough advanced preparation to know what his company's strategic priority was.

The Way to Go

George C. Marshall was always a step or more ahead of his peers and his opponents. In the 1920s, he was preparing America's future generals; in the 1930s, he was striving valiantly to prepare America for war; and in 1940, he had his staff working on the possibility of a global war with Germany. However, one of his more amazing feats of preparation occurred in 1943, while America was engaged in a bitter struggle with Germany in Europe and Japan in the Pacific. Marshall not only had the foresight to anticipate victory over both opponents, he had the wisdom to prepare for the difficult work that would follow after the victory. He therefore ordered that a division of civil affairs be established within the army, and he charged it with planning and preparing for the postwar occupation of both Germany and Japan. He informed his staff that the army's success in the vanquished countries after the war would go a long way toward preventing the conditions that created the two previous world wars and thus significantly reduce the possibility of a future conflict.

Marshall's foresight stands in contrast to the situation the U.S. military faced in 2003, after the fall of Baghdad, when public and private institutions alike were looted and destroyed because no comprehensive plan had been put in place in advance of the anticipated victory. As violence and casualties escalated throughout 2004, the lack of preparation had even more tragic consequences.

In his quiet way, Marshall understood that it is just as important to prepare for peace in the middle of a war as it was to prepare for war in times of peace. It might sound paradoxical, but the principle of preparation demands that one never stop preparing for the future.

SHARING KNOWLEDGE

The Principle of Learning and Teaching

[The Army] found in Marshall one of those rare teachers who made a difference, who open minds in such a way that they never afterwards quite close again or forget the excitement of a new idea.

—Forrest Pogue

I learned how to learn.

—George C. Marshall, commenting on his time at
the Army Infantry and Cavalry School

☆ ☆ ☆ ☆ ☆

In the summer of 1925, an army lieutenant went out to observe the Fifteenth Infantry, then under the command of Lieutenant Colonel George Marshall, in a ten-day field exercise. The young officer noted that after the first squad completed its exercise, Marshall made a general critique of their performance before the entire squad. He then drew the squad leader aside and made more pointed remarks—noting a series of errors, mistakes, and oversights. The lieutenant was surprised when, after the first exercise, Marshall didn't pass off the responsibility to a more junior officer. He grew even more astounded when Marshall remained throughout the entire ten-day exercise and critiqued and instructed every single unit. Afterward, the officer recalled feeling that the exercise was "a great comedown" because he began to wonder what the army held for him when, a decade after the First World War, Marshall—one of that war's "large figures" and a man who had overseen complex operations consisting of over 600,000 troops—"was busily engaged in teaching little groups of eight to ten men how to handle themselves on the field." Only later did the officer come to realize that what Marshall was demonstrating was not a weakness but a strength.[1]

George Marshall was, above all else, a teacher. He understood that it was his job to not only train his regiment but to share his experience and knowledge as well. Moreover, he realized that those responsibilities could not be delegated. It is this under-standing that lies at the heart of Marshall's sixth leadership prin-ciple, sharing knowledge—the principle of learning and teaching.

Learning How to Learn: A History of Learning

Every great teacher is also a great learner. George Marshall was no exception. Forrest Pogue, Marshall's biographer, wrote that at the turn of the twentieth century no civilian or military insti-tution "provided proper grounding" for high command, thus any enterprising officer had to train himself. "And for this," Pogue added, "he needed a belief in himself, an intense desire to know, the capacity to grow, the trait of self-discipline, and a compulsion to excel in his chosen field."[2]

Many other officers of the era also shared Marshall's self-confidence, self-discipline, and "compulsion to excel," but it was his "intense desire to know" that separated Marshall from his peers.

This characteristic was not self-evident in Marshall from the beginning. In fact, as a child, Marshall was a mediocre stu-dent who had been turned off to learning by an overbearing aunt who practiced a very dry and staid approach to education. Throughout high school and college (and with the exception of history classes), Marshall could best be described as an average student.

It was not until 1906 when he was accepted to the Army Infantry and Cavalry School at Fort Leavenworth and had to compete with more senior officers that he finally began applying himself to the task of studying. As he later said, "It was the hardest work I ever did in my life." The effort paid off because not only did Marshall—the most junior officer at the school at the time—graduate first in his class, he "finally got into the habit of study." Even more important, it was here that Marshall said he "learned how to learn." It was a trait that would remain with him for the rest of his life.

A great deal of credit for Marshall's newfound appreciation for self-education goes to Major John F. Morrison, an instructor at Leavenworth at the time. A brilliant teacher, Morrison approached military problems from the school of applied thought as opposed to the old doctrine that emphasized the "language of regulations."[3] He also stressed the themes of simplicity and self-education. All of these characteristics would later manifest themselves in Marshall's own approach to teaching.

In the immediate years after Leavenworth, Marshall's newfound appreciation for learning became evident as he deliberately set tasks for which he had no special aptitude. For instance, after he purchased his first car—a Model T Ford—Marshall was compelled by his curiosity to disassemble the engine. And in spite of not being "at all mechanical," he familiarized himself with the workings of the internal combustion engine. Marshall learned Chinese during his tour of duty in Tientsin and became proficient enough in the language to transcribe the testimony of a Chinese man during a court hearing. And in 1938, as chief of the War Plans Division, he conducted a nationwide air tour for the sole purpose of learning more about air power.

Even during the war years, when the responsibilities that befell him were of such a magnitude that it would have been forgivable if Marshall had found little time for anything else, he refused to stop learning. He understood his job demanded constant learning.

One of the less important—but more telling—stories of Marshall's wonderful approach to learning occurred in the early days of 1945, when he was visiting American troops in Europe. At the time, Winston Churchill was hoping to exploit Allied advances in Europe and decided to again press the issue of an advance into the Balkans. Marshall was opposed to the idea but feared he lacked the specific information to counter Churchill's suggestion that the advance was feasible. During a haircut—given to him by an Italian prisoner of war—Marshall learned that the barber had grown up in the very region through which the British were hoping the allies could advance into the Balkans. By the time his haircut was done, Marshall had so thoroughly quizzed the barber (and another prisoner) that his new knowledge of the mountainous region confirmed his concerns. Later that day, he used his new information to defeat the objections of his British counterparts. Marshall later recalled with some satisfaction that the British were amazed by his detailed knowledge of the area.[4]

Applying the Lessons of History

As a young boy, Marshall was a mediocre student but, as he later said, "I could star in history." It was just a passing comment he made in the twilight of his life, yet a cursory review of Marshall's career shows that he not only had a lifelong fascination with history, he possessed a remarkable skill for not only applying the lessons of history but getting others to also absorb the lessons of history. Richard Neustadt, in his book *Thinking in Time*, ranks Marshall as one of the best leaders of the twentieth century in the art of using history to constructively think about the future.

Little is known about the historical books or figures Marshall studied as a young man, but during his time at the Virginia Military Institute he received large doses of American military history and became intimately familiar with the events and personalities of the Revolutionary War and the Civil War. As a young officer, Marshall studied the Spanish-American War of 1898 and, at Fort Leavenworth, he studied Henri de Jomini and Carl von Clausewitz and other great military strategists. And, as a participant in World War I, Marshall learned firsthand many of the lessons of that war. All in all, he was thoroughly grounded in the history of warfare.

One of the earliest examples of Marshall applying these lessons of history is found in a 1923 speech he was asked to give on short notice to the annual meeting of the Military Schools and Colleges Association. He began by citing the history of the Revolutionary War. "There are but a few men today who have even a vague idea of Washington's troubles in maintaining his Revolutionary Army," he said, reminding them that at one point the American army had been reduced to less than a hundred soldiers. He then retold of the crisis that occurred shortly before the start of the Mexican War, when General Winfield Scott's army "was well nigh emasculated and rendered impotent by the policy of the government, which permitted a large proportion of the volunteers to secure their discharges and return home." Next, he pointed out how the Union's lack of a professional army in 1860 prevented it from putting down the South's rebellion before it grew into a civil war. He then related his own experience in World War I—of soldiers going without boots and having to wrap their feet in gunnysacks. He concluded by recounting an eerie coincidence pointed out to him by General John J. Pershing: At the end of the war, Pershing noted, there were English soldiers located in Cologne, American soldiers at Coblenz, and French soldiers in Mayence. He then reminded Marshall that 1,800 years before, Roman legions were also stationed at Cologne, Coblenz, and Mayence in Germany, and he concluded by saying that "there must be some lesson to be drawn from this repetition of history."

Later, as chief of staff, Marshall would in fact draw the lessons from each of these war experiences. The first lesson was that there was an inherent risk in allowing the army to reduce too greatly in size. At a minimum, it prevented quick action—like the Union's inability to repress the South—and, at worse, it encouraged aggression. In every instance—in the Revolutionary War, the Civil War, and the First World War—casualties and costs were higher than they otherwise would have been had the U.S. Army been better prepared. It was this lesson that prompted Marshall—in the years between 1939 and 1941—to fight so hard to get America better prepared.

Marshall also drew direct parallels between the U.S. government allowing troops to return home before the Mexican War and his situation in the summer of 1941, when Congress was considering allowing the first group of draftees to be discharged just as war appeared imminent. He understood that the politically expedient act had very nearly cost America a victory in the war, and he was not about to let it happen again.

The lessons of America's involvement in the war in Cuba, which he studied as a second lieutenant, also stuck with Marshall. He knew that the United States was so ill-prepared before that war that soldiers often had to wear winter wool uniforms in the tropical heat and that more Americans died in that conflict from disease and illness (due to a shortage of supplies and medicine) than they did of wounds received in the battle. As chief of staff, he ensured that those lessons were neither forgotten, nor repeated.

It was, however, the lessons of World War I that Marshall most consistently applied. From direct experience, he knew that it had taken more than a full year before American forces were finally able to fight in World War I—and even then they did so with no American manufactured ammunition and only 1,000 planes (out of an estimated 50,000 airplanes the country had expected to produce). Marshall never let the president, Congress, and the American people forget these "lessons from history"—although they often refused to listen until it was almost too late.

The Student Becomes the Teacher

During Marshall's second tour of duty in the Philippines (1913–1916), the army reached "low ebb." It was a skeleton organization and its officer corps was undermanned, underpaid, and lacked a method for promoting its most qualified officers. Marshall, then only a first lieutenant, had a group of ten young officers under him, all of whom were nearing the end of their three-year tour of duty and suffering from low morale. Marshall, who always felt that morale flowed from the top, resolved to do something about the situation. His solution was to voluntarily organize an officer school—with himself as its only instructor. He requested that the officers attend each morning and began sharing the vast amount of knowledge he had absorbed from his years at the Army Command and General Staff College and, more recently, as an aide to a general. One of the officers later wrote that "none of us who participated ever forgot it," and added that it was "just a small incident in the life of a great man, but it show[ed] his flair for real leadership in an instance when his students really had to be shown."[5]

It was hardly the only instance. Throughout his career, Marshall assumed the role of teacher. At the end of World War I, when U.S. soldiers were growing agitated at not being allowed to return home, Marshall went on a lecture circuit to educate American soldiers on their battlefield accomplishments. His rationale was that if the troops understood the scope and magnitude of their accomplishments, "their pride in past achievement would stiffen them against their present discontent."[6]

It was, however, in China in the mid-1920s that Marshall received his greatest motivation to become a teacher. Upon first arriving in the country, he wrote Pershing and said, "I find the officers are highly developed in the technical handling or functioning of weapons . . . and in the special and intricate details of paperwork or administration generally; but when it comes to simple tactical problems, the actual details of leading troops, they all fall below the standards they set in other matters."

The point was driven home during a field exercise outside Tientsin. He encountered a young graduate of Fort Benning (the U.S. Army's top infantry school) struggling to write a long and verbose field order—the type he had been taught by army doctrine to draft up. By the time the soldier was done with the job, the tactical opportunity for attacking the enemy had passed. Marshall was horrified and later said, "The man was no fool . . . but he had been taught an absurd system." He resolved then and there "to get my hands on Benning" and change the system.[7]

In fact, Marshall didn't even wait until he returned to the United States to start making changes. On his way back from his three-year tour, Marshall began holding seminars for the other returning officers on the *practical* lessons of the First World War.

Studying the First Six Months

In one of his first lectures at Fort Benning, Marshall laid out in practical terms how he intended to remake the curriculum. He began:

> Picture the opening campaign of a war. It is a cloud of uncertainty, haste, rapid movements, congestion on the roads, strange terrain, lack of ammunition and supplies at the right place at the right moment, failures of communications, terrific tests of endurance, and misunderstandings in direct proportion to the inexperience of the officers and the aggressive action of the enemy. Add to this a minimum of preliminary information of the enemy and

of his dispositions, poor maps, and a speed of movement . . . resulting from fast-flying planes, fast-moving tanks, armored cars, and motor transportation in general. There you have warfare of movement such as swept over Belgium or Northern France in 1914, but at far greater speed. That, gentlemen, is what you are suppose to be preparing for.

To stress his point, Marshall made students work with foreign maps and out-of-date road maps because they more accurately corresponded to the resources soldiers would likely have in the opening months of a war. A student of Marshall's, later a general in World War II, said: "He was so right, because that's exactly what we had—maps of North Africa were no good, and as far as the Pacific was concerned, if you got a sketch you were lucky." The man added, "I have never forgotten [his] dictum . . . study the first six months of the next war."[8]

Next, Marshall systematically demolished the school's old teaching style, which focused on "solutions," and replaced it with one that emphasized initiative and independent thought. So crucial was the latter characteristic that Marshall would publish any student's work that showed "a flair for the unorthodox."

To encourage fast and independent thinking, Marshall engaged his students in an almost endless series of brain-teasing games. He would distribute books on history, sociology, psychology, and a variety of other topics in an effort to get his students to think differently. He knew from his past experience in World War I that if the army "had fought by the book rules, we would have wrecked ourselves about every twenty minutes." A textbook written under his tenure at Benning captured this point. It read: "The art of war has no traffic rules … for the infinitely varied circumstances and conditions of combat never produce the same situation twice."[9]

Even long after he left Benning, Marshall continued to stress these themes. To a class of graduates at Fort Benning on the eve of World War II, he said, "Warfare today . . . is a thing of swift movement—of rapid concentrations . . . it is not a game for the unimaginative plodder."

Marshall's time at Benning was well spent. In total, it is believed he instructed or worked with 200 officers who later served as generals in World War II. One of those generals, Omar Bradley, who went on to great fame in the war and was later the last five-star general in U.S. history, paid him perhaps the ultimate compliment when he said of Marshall, "I learned from him the rudiments of effective command."

Directing Men

One of George Marshall's more famous comments came from his time at Fort Benning when he implored his instructors to "direct men by trying to make them see the way to go." A few examples from his career demonstrate what he had in mind.

In early 1941, before the Japanese attacked Pearl Harbor and America was still neutral, two officers came to Marshall with a plan to occupy the Cape Verde Islands in a preemptive attack designed to prevent Germany from occupying the strategic islands in the Atlantic Ocean. Marshall called the officers into his office and asked them to put themselves in his place—and he would play the role of the president. He then asked the officers to "explain to me briefly and clearly why you propose to launch an attack upon the property of a neutral?" The two officers groped for an answer and were saved a stern lecture only because Marshall was called away by an emergency. The implication of his question, however, was clear: The officers had not thought through their plan, and by merely asking a tough, pointed question, Marshall was able to make his point.[10]

Marshall once did the same thing to Maxwell Taylor, who later served as chief of staff of the U.S. Army and was recalled to active duty during the Kennedy administration to serve as chairman of the Joint Chiefs of Staff. When he was a young officer on Marshall's staff, Taylor presented him with a paper that outlined a disagreement between two of Marshall's assistant chiefs of staff. Marshall asked Taylor what he thought his decision should be. Taylor replied, "Sir, I hadn't thought about it." "Please do so," replied Marshall. It was all the instruction Taylor ever needed. Never again did he go see "the boss" without having formed an opinion.[11]

Marshall also made the president "see the way to go" as required. Early on in his tenure as chief of staff, Marshall was having a difficult time explaining the army's new organization plans to President Roosevelt. Knowing that the president was a former assistant secretary of navy, Marshall decided to cut out a huge diagram in the shape of a ship. On the bow, he designed the army's new triangular division structure, in the middle of the ship were three squares to represent the National Guard divisions, and at the stern were the support elements.

Marshall always made it a point to teach people in terms they could readily grasp.

Even in his final days as secretary of state, Marshall was still teaching. He happened to be in Bogotá, Colombia when rebel forces seized the city's radio stations and began broadcasting appeals for revolution. Fighting quickly broke out and the local officials responsible for protecting Marshall soon became concerned for his safety and sent a small contingent of Colombian soldiers to the house where Marshall was staying. The soldiers took up their position at the front entrance. Marshall watched the scene unfold for a few minutes and then asked the officer in charge what would happen if rebels came to the back door. The officer provided no answer. "If I remember my small-unit tactics correctly," Marshall gently instructed, "when you are defending a perimeter, what you do is to garrison that perimeter lightly and place a large, centrally located, mobile reserve at a point where it can move rapidly to any threatened point on the perimeter." Thus, even to the end, Marshall was a teacher.

Lessons: In His Own Words

"Direct men by trying to make them see the way to go." The strength of the U.S. Army, Marshall knew, rested less on his individual talents and more on those of everyone around him. It was why he desired to "get his hands" on Fort Benning—one of the army's premier training schools.

In 1996, Roger Enrico, then CEO of PepsiCo, started his own "war college" to train and develop the next generation of company leaders. Enrico dedicated months to the job and trained more than a hundred senior managers. A number of other prominent CEOs have done the same thing. Bob Nardelli, CEO of The Home Depot, started the Home Depot Store Leadership Program. David Neeleman, CEO of JetBlue Airways, teaches his "Principles of Leadership." And David Novak, Chairman and CEO of YUM! Brands, Inc., has instructed more than 600 of his executives. As Jeffrey Immelt, CEO of General Electric Company, recently said, "A leader's primary role is to teach. People who work with you . . . have to feel you're willing to share what you've learned."

Effective leaders understand that if their organization is to grow, it is essential that they have leaders in place to sustain that growth—which means they need to take the lead in training the next generation of leaders.

"What do you think my decision should be?" This is the question Marshall asked Maxwell Taylor when he was just a young officer. Taylor's inability to provide an answer was a lesson he never forgot. When he was CEO of GE, Jack Welch often posed this question to students at GE's Crotonville training facility (now the John F. Welch School of Leadership): "If you were named CEO of GE tomorrow, what would you do?"

Such questions do more than simply prepare future leaders; they help subordinates to connect to the realities that the CEO has to deal with on a daily basis. And that, in turn, fosters an environment in which everyone in the company is thinking of ways to solve problems and exploit new opportunities.

Marshall used this approach to mentor Eisenhower, Bradley, and Taylor (among others), and a number of other modern

CEOs have done the same thing. Jack Welch was instrumental in the careers of former GE executives who have gone on to become CEOs: Bob Nardelli (The Home Depot), Jim McNerney (3M Company), and Tom Tiller (Polaris Industries). Dick Cooley, the former CEO of Wells Fargo, did much the same thing with his executives: Jerry Grundhofer (U.S. Bancorp), Frank Newman (Bankers Trust), Richard Rosenberg (Bank of America), and Bob Joss (Westpac Banking).[12] The bottom line is that great leaders create other great leaders—and they do it through teaching.

"Expunge the bunk, complications, and ponderosities." Throughout his career, Marshall mandated simplicity. As a staff officer, he understood that if orders were not prepared in an easy-to-understand manner and issued quickly enough to be implemented, they were worthless. As an instructor, he stressed that lessons had to be delivered in such a way that soldiers could instantly comprehend the issue and execute the required action. To emphasize this point, he stipulated to his officers, "We must get down to the essentials, make clear the real difficulties, and expunge the bunk, complications, and ponderosities . . . [w]e must develop a technique and method so simple and so brief that the citizen officer of good common sense can readily grasp the idea."

Peter Drucker once eloquently captured this same point when he asked each member of the board of directors of ServiceMaster what the company's core business was. After receiving a variety of answers, Drucker told them they were all wrong. He said their business was "to train the least-skilled people and make them functional." To do that, teaching has to be conducted in such a manner that the lessons can be readily and efficiently absorbed by everyone in the organization.

"We will repeat our errors of the past unless public opinion is enlightened." George Marshall believed that one of the best—and easiest—ways to prepare for the future was to study and apply the lessons of history. For instance, Marshall often used vivid historical examples of important themes that seemed to play themselves over and over again. An unwillingness to invest and a failure to prepare were two of these recurring themes. One company that learned the consequences of such failures is Intel Corporation. In the early 1990s, a math professor discovered a problem in one of Intel's new chips. Since the problem occurred only during complex mathematical operations, Intel refused to address the problem because it affected only a small number of people. But then the math professor began to contact some of his colleagues, and soon Intel's refusal to deal with the problem turned into a huge public relations disaster. In the end, the chipmaker not only had to correct the problem, it had to recall every chip (even though most users weren't affected) at a cost of $475 million. Having learned its lesson, Intel now deals with all problems in a quick, efficient, and forthright manner.

"Study the first six months of the next war." While Marshall was extraordinarily gifted at using history to guide his actions, he refused to fall prey to the idea that events would unfold in precisely the same way. This was particularly true with regard to how technology would change warfare. Marshall understood it would reduce the time America had to prepare for war; magnify

the speed at which war progressed; and increase the destructive power of modern weapons.

One modern CEO who seems to embrace this approach is the former CEO of Intel, Craig Barrett. In an interview in late 2003, Barrett said:

> The dimensions that we operate at today in building transistors are precisely the dimensions of DNA and proteins. So if I just let my imagination run wild for a minute, what I'm really interested in is bringing the economics and accuracy of what we do . . . to the health science side.

In short, Barrett was saying that Intel—a semiconductor company—needed to start playing in the health care field. By studying the future, Barrett not only identified a new and potentially lucrative market for Intel, he sent a message that he expected his officers and employees to begin learning about this new area.[13]

"If we had fought by the book rules, we would have wrecked ourselves about every twenty minutes." Marshall constantly emphasized the need for independent thought, initiative, and flexibility because he understood open warfare was going to be "the rule rather than the exception." One way he tried to drill this message home was by publishing examples of work that "ran counter to the approved school solution." A second way he demonstrated this belief was by being open to learning from anywhere—and everything.

Earlier in this chapter I recounted the story of how Marshall learned about the Balkan terrain from an Italian prisoner of war. A number of successful CEOs have adopted a similar strategy of learning from almost anything. For instance, Bill Pollard, CEO of ServiceMaster during the 1980s, once stated that he got "ideas from helping to start a project in an Indian village in Ecuador."[14] Jack Welch recalls a story of having dinner with two plant managers from Brazil and the United Kingdom, both of whom had achieved annual inventory turns of 33 and 40 days, respectively. Welch quizzed them about their tools, social architecture, and even how they overcame a resistance to a new methodology. He then used the information to double GE's inventory turns.[15]

I learned how to learn. The importance of lifelong learning is so obvious that it hardly seems worth repeating, yet because it is so essential, it bears repeating. In the book *True Leaders*, Jack Kahl, the founder of Manco, Inc., recounts the story of watching Secretariat win the third leg of the Triple Crown in 1973. Afterward, Kahl said he broke down and cried because he realized that in winning by over thirty lengths, Secretariat was not competing against anyone else—only himself. The horse's powerful performance thus served as an important lesson, and Kahl vowed at that moment to "be as good as I could be." That commitment caused him to embrace learning because it made him a better person.[16]

Marshall also understood that to "cease mental development" would not only have been harmful to his prospects for advancement in the army, it could have been deadly to the security of the nation he had taken an oath to protect. During his lifetime, Marshall witnessed the introduction of the car, the tank, the radio, the airplane, and the atomic bomb. It was vital that he embrace lifelong learning in order to understand how these new technologies were going to change his job.

The challenge for today's business leader is no less daunting. The pace of knowledge is said to double every seven years, and the shelf life of most PhDs is now less than five years. Biotechnology, nanotechnology, DNA analysis, computer speed, broadband—all these technology developments are growing at exponential rates, and it is essential that today's leaders embrace learning and remain open to new technologies and new ideas. The future, as Marshall would remind us, is not a game for the "unimaginative plodder."

The Way to Go

George C. Marshall's entire adult life was spent in service to his country. However, for a brief time after he graduated from Virginia Military Institute and before he earned his commission in the army, Marshall served as a teacher at the Danville Military Institute in Virginia. It wasn't really a surprising choice because, as his biographer Forrest Pogue wrote, "Marshall had an unusual talent as a teacher . . . and he himself sometimes regretted that he had not set out on an academic career.[17]

In retrospect, there is no reason Marshall should have regretted his choice because in almost every position he ever occupied he taught those around him. This is best demonstrated in a speech Marshall gave to students at Princeton University in

1947. In his address, he said he doubted "whether a man can think with full wisdom and with deep convictions regarding . . . the basic issues today who has not at least reviewed in his mind the period of the Peloponnesian War and the fall of Athens."

As a leader, Marshall knew it was his responsibility to get the next generation to understand that the United States' leadership in the world—while secure at the moment—could just as easily go the way of Athens. Moreover, he understood that it was his responsibility to ingrain that lesson in the next generation.

Warren Bennis once wrote that "[l]eaders are, by definition, innovators. They do things other people haven't done or don't do. They do things in advance of other people. They make new things. They make old things new. *Having learned from the past, they live in the present, with one eye on the future.*"[18] George Marshall would have undoubtedly concurred, and he may well have added that the only way a leader can do all of those things is by learning and teaching others.

CHOOSING AND REWARDING THE RIGHT PEOPLE
The Principle of Fairness

The strongest weapon that I always had in my hand was a confident feeling that you trusted my judgment.
— General Dwight D. Eisenhower, in a letter of
appreciation to Marshall after V-E Day

I am awfully tired of seeing mediocrity placed in high positions.
— George C. Marshall

$\star$ $\star$ $\star$ $\star$ $\star$

The list of people who served under George Marshall reads like a "who's who" of famous soldiers and civilians. There are the legendary American generals during the Second World War, among them Dwight D. Eisenhower, George Patton, Douglas MacArthur, Omar Bradley, J. Lawton Collins, Walter Bedell Smith, Lucian Truscott, Maxwell Taylor, Mark Clark, and Matthew Ridgway. Then there are the influential diplomats in the early days of the Cold War: Dean Acheson, Dean Rusk, George Kennan, Robert Lovett, and Charles Bohlen.

The list could go on. In fact, it is so extensive that it has given rise to one of the more enduring myths surrounding George Marshall, which is that he had a "little black book" that he supposedly used to keep track of promising individuals. So pervasive is the myth that it is recounted in nearly every biography or book written about Marshall—including Forrest Pogue's four-volume biography (widely considered to be the bible on George Marshall).

The truth is that no such book existed. The myth was started by General James Van Fleet, who cited the existence of the book as the reason he was not promoted more rapidly during World War II. Van Fleet claimed Marshall confused his name with an officer of a similar-sounding name—but of lesser ability—and incorrectly jotted it down in his "little black book." The story was accepted by Pogue and included in his biography and has been repeated ever since. Pogue later acknowledged his error and admitted he did not verify the story. Subsequently, no record of the infamous "little black book" has ever been found.

The lack of such a book only serves to heighten one's appreciation for Marshall's unique skill in picking the right people, because it suggests he made it a priority to find other ways to keep tabs on and promote qualified individuals. Marshall's seventh leadership principle—the principle of fairness—stems from his remarkable abilities in this area.

A History of Spotting—and Promoting—Talent

Whenever the issue of Marshall's legendary talent for promoting meritorious individuals is discussed, the case of Dwight D. Eisenhower is cited. At the beginning of World War II, Marshall "jumped" Eisenhower—then a lieutenant colonel—over 350 more senior officers and promoted him to the rank of brigadier general. It is a great example, but the case of Omar Bradley is even more telling. As Forrest Pogue remarked, "Bradley was likely to be overlooked by anyone giving a quick appraisal of a group of potential leaders.[1] Unlike Eisenhower, Bradley did not radiate charm, and his quiet style was nearly the complete opposite of a MacArthur or Patton. And yet Marshall saw enough in Bradley during a few short encounters at Fort Benning to consistently give him greater responsibilities and promote him whenever he proved he was ready for the next step—including advancing him over his one-time commander, George Patton. As Bradley's career demonstrated, he was worthy of Marshall's support. In 1951, he became chairman of the Joint Chiefs of Staff and was the last military officer to have obtained the five stars.

Another young officer who caught Marshall's attention was J. Lawton Collins. A decade after Marshall had met him at Fort Benning, Collins—still only a major after seventeen years with the military—wrote Marshall a letter expressing discouragement and doubts about the viability of his future prospects in the army. Marshall promptly wrote him back and gave him some much-needed hope. The army, he said, will be "showing signs of real modernization when they reach down and pick you and several others of your stripe, which I imagine will be done, and shortly." Three years later Marshall, as chief of staff, made good on that prediction, and by 1942, Collins was a major general. And like Bradley, Collins went on to a distinguished career as a combat leader in the war and later served as chief of staff of the army during the Korean War.

Marshall's penchant for spotting and promoting talent was by no means limited to the officer corps. Toward the end of the war, as the need for an ever-greater number of junior officers became apparent, Marshall demanded that merit be given primary consideration and insisted that at least 50 percent of the vacancies in the junior-officer ranks be given to enlisted personnel who distinguished themselves through outstanding performance.

The best testimony of Marshall's belief in the principle of fairness, however, occurred in 1950 after he became secretary of defense. Faced once again with rebuilding an army, Marshall knew his top priority was to increase military manpower and strength. To solve the issue, he turned to the most qualified person in the country to serve as assistant secretary of defense for manpower. That person was Anna Rosenberg. She was a controversial choice, not only because she was a woman, but because she was a Jew, the daughter of a Hungarian immigrant, and a liberal New Dealer. Marshall, however, knew she had a vast amount of experience and had served with distinction in both the private sector and later in the government during the Second World War as a member of the War Manpower Commission. As noted in Chapter One, when Joseph McCarthy falsely accused her of harboring communist sympathies, Marshall stood by her side until she was confirmed because he knew she was the best person for the job.

Making Talent Assessment a Priority

Part of Marshall's success stems from the simple fact that in the early days of the U.S. Army, the ranks of the professional officer corps was small enough that Marshall personally knew many of the officers—or at least their reputations—and could assess their talent. But this was true for any officer. What made Marshall special was that he worked at the job and made it a priority.

In the early 1920s, Marshall served on a committee to review the service records of the entire army officer corps. It was long, tedious, and often boring work, but he did it, in part, because he was interested in investigating whether there were inequities in the promotion system (he wanted to find a better way to promote talent) and, in part, because he wanted to familiarize himself with all of the army officers' records. As was noted earlier, Marshall was ambitious in terms of his professional aspirations, and he realized that his success along the way would rest, in large measure, on those officers with whom he surrounded himself. To the extent possible, he was determined—as a commanding officer—to get the best junior officers available.

This characteristic was accentuated when he became chief of staff. One of his first acts was to order a systematic overhaul of the army's outdated promotion system. With war on the horizon, Marshall knew his ability to personally keep track of and promote qualified officers would be severely limited by the sheer size of the army, so he wanted a system that would permit him "to put [his] finger on the men" he wanted.

But Marshall knew that he had to do even more than develop a better system. He realized he needed to be able to rapidly promote individuals like Eisenhower, Bradley, Collins, and scores of other promising young officers. His answer was "an innocuous-sounding" amendment that he had the wisdom to push into law in 1940. The amendment read, "In time of war or national emergency . . . any officer of the Regular Army may be appointed to higher temporary grade without vacating his permanent appointment." It essentially allowed Marshall to make vacancies for qualified junior officers and promote them at his discretion. According to at least one historian, the act "may well have been Marshall's greatest contribution to the United States Army" because it permitted him to bypass a number of senior army officers whom he considered "deadwood" and place in their stead capable officers who were up for the rigors of modern warfare.[2]

Sometimes Marshall simply exercised common sense and his penchant for action in promoting good people. Marshall once told General Charles Corlett how it was that he had come to be selected as a general officer. "I did not know you," said Marshall, "I was aware that you were in command of the Thirtieth Infantry, but little else. I came down to my office one morning and, going through my mail, I found five requests for you by senior officers." He said he immediately called the personnel department and instructed them to make Corlett a general.[3]

Promoting, Delegating, and Supporting

While it is unquestionable that the principle of basic fairness was at the heart of Marshall's rationale for promoting people, he also did it for a more basic reason: Promoting qualified people made his job easier and, more important, enhanced the prospects for the success of the army and the nation during the war. As a leader, however, Marshall recognized that his job didn't stop there. He understood that talented people could only perform to their full potential if he delegated authority to them, then supported them when they exercised that authority.

Marshall's philosophy in this regard was best captured in a response he once gave to a well-wisher who had congratulated him on the victory in North Africa. In his typical self-effacing style, Marshall said it was quite easy: Just "pick the right man for the job and back him up with every resource at our disposal."[4]

And if Omar Bradley is the epitome of Marshall's ability to assess and promote talent, Dwight Eisenhower remains the best example of how he delegated and supported individuals under his command. Shortly before promoting Eisenhower to his senior command position, Marshall granted him great authority when he said he "must have assistants who will solve their problems and tell me later what they have done." In short, he was telling Eisenhower that he expected him to act in his best judgment and get the job done.

And when Eisenhower did exercise his authority, Marshall supported him to the hilt. During the fighting in North Africa, Eisenhower got into a good deal of trouble because he permitted Admiral Jean Darlan to take command of the French forces. Darlan was a controversial leader because he had earlier held a prominent position in the pro-German Vichy government. The ensuing political crisis threatened Eisenhower's position (opponents felt his selection not only ran counter to the allies' commitment to democracy, but was also a slap in the face to those French who had bravely resisted the Germans). Marshall, however, never wavered in his support of Eisenhower. He understood that his subordinate took the measure as a way of saving American lives. As one commentator later said of the decision, it helped ensure that French guns were pointed at the German forces instead of at the allies. Marshall told Eisenhower not to "waste his brain power" on the matter and said he would support him "in every possible way."

Marshall continued to support Eisenhower, even after the victory in North Africa was achieved. In the days leading up to D-Day, Marshall offered Eisenhower his unyielding support and informed him that he need only list his "final desires and so far as I can see . . . they will be approved."

The full extent of Marshall's support for Eisenhower was best displayed during the critical months of late 1944 and early 1945, when it appeared that an aggressive German counterattack in the Ardennes had stalled his advance. A less trusting or supportive superior would have felt the need to get involved, but Marshall refused to question or judge Eisenhower's actions, saying only that he felt "the commander in the field is the best judge." Marshall knew Eisenhower's skills and capabilities, and his trust in him was borne out when Eisenhower successfully beat back the counteroffensive and regained the initiative.

Marshall's approach to delegating authority and supporting subordinates can best be summed by this simple statement of his: "We, in headquarters, live . . . in order that people in the field may carry out their orders." Early in the war, in April 1942, to drive home this point to his staff in Washington, D.C., Marshall sent a short memorandum that read:

> At a dinner for me in London, the head of the British Administrative Service read for our amusement a letter that had come to his attention, written by the Duke of Wellington from Spain in about 1810 to the Secretary of State for War, Lord Bradford. I asked for a copy and quote it below for our guidance in the present struggle.
>
> *"My Lord,*
>
> *"If I attempted to answer the mass of futile correspondence that surrounds me, I should be debarred from all serious business of campaigning.*

"I must remind your Lordship—for the last time—that so long as I retain an independent position, I shall see that no officer under my Command is debarred by attending to the futile driveling of mere quill driving in your Lordship's office—from attending to his first duty—which is, and has always been, so to train the private men under his command that they may, without question, beat any force opposed to them in the field.

"I am,

> *My Lord,*
>> *Your Obedient Servant,*
>>> *Wellington."*

Marshall then added this postscript to the message:

> The reaction to instructions from Washington of a troop commander far from home, in surroundings which we are utterly unfamiliar, may be akin to those of the Great Duke, and we could well govern ourselves accordingly.
>
> G. C. Marshall
> Chief of Staff[5]

And Marshall and his staff did govern themselves accordingly and, in the process, demonstrated that one of the hallmarks of effective leadership is simply supporting the people to whom the task of getting the job done has been delegated.

At the conclusion of the war in Europe, Eisenhower said that his "strongest weapon" in defeating the enemy was always Marshall's support.

Loyalty

Another hallmark of Marshall's leadership was his unbending loyalty. While his integrity would not allow him to keep unqualified or underperforming subordinates in their positions, Marshall was secure enough in his qualified judgment of people to support them when they made honest mistakes or were unfairly attacked by others.

In critical battles MacArthur had with the navy on the issue of overall command in the Pacific, Marshall always supported his subordinate. When the navy questioned the wisdom of allowing MacArthur to return to the Philippines (to keep his "I shall return" promise), Marshall went to bat in his favor. Twice, he came to the rescue of General Joseph Stilwell when powerful forces within China and the White House—including President Roosevelt himself—suggested Stilwell be removed from his position as deputy supreme allied commander of the Southeast Asia command and Chiang Kai-shek's chief of staff. (Ultimately, however, Stilwell's strong personality and quick tongue—his nickname was "Vinegar Joe"—proved even too much for Marshall and he had to relieve him.) Marshall even supported General George Patton in a confrontation with Admiral Ernest King, the navy's top officer, who had grown so weary of battling Patton for resources that he asked Marshall to relieve him. Marshall refused King's request, saying that the same qualities that made Patton so difficult to work with were the same qualities that were so useful on the battlefield.

The more telling demonstrations of Marshall's loyalty, however, occurred not in his dealing with the powerful but rather in his dealings with subordinates—far removed from the spotlight. Once a senior military attaché serving under Marshall's command was accused by the Roosevelt White House of being a traitor and a spy (supposedly because he harbored isolationist and pro-German views). Marshall queried the man's immediate superior, General Miles Sherman, the army head of intelligence, and asked if it was true. Sherman replied by saying that "no man here is so valuable if he worries you. Let me get rid of him." Marshall refused the invitation to make his life easier and responded by asking Sherman if the attaché was a good man and still useful. Told he was, Marshall informed Sherman: "If you need him . . . I will tell the White House." As Hap Arnold, general of the U.S. Army Air Corps, once said of Marshall, "He was always loyal."

Valuing Everyone

The secret of George Marshall's success when it came to spotting and promoting talent is difficult to assess. Part of his success lay in his ability to overlook certain weaknesses. For instance, Marshall deplored Patton's love of violence, his profanity, and his swaggering showmanship, but at the same time he realized that in war those same characteristics could be extremely valuable. Part of his success was due to his willingness to knock down bureaucratic barriers to keep and promote talented officers. One story has Marshall fighting against the military bureaucracy to ensure that a young, capable officer who happened to be color-blind was allowed to stay in the army. (Marshall won that battle.) A third element of his success rested on supporting subordinates who demonstrated characteristics he favored, even if they did not always meet with the universal support of others, including their peers, their own subordinates, or their superiors.

The largest measure of his success, however, stemmed from the simple fact that Marshall realized everyone, at some level, had merit. And he realized it was his job as a leader to assess their merit and then give them an appropriate amount of responsibility. During the graduation ceremonies for the United States Military Academy in 1942, Marshall patiently received every graduate, and when the last cadet—typically the student with the lowest academic standing—came onstage, he grabbed the young man's hand and raised it high in the air, declaring to the approval of the audience, "In this war we need less mathematics and more powder." It was his way of saying that everyone had value.

Lessons: In His Own Words

"I am awfully tired of seeing mediocrity placed in high positions, with brilliance and talent damned by lack of rank to obscurity." George Marshall promoted scores of talented junior officers ahead of senior officers. One of those individuals, Dwight Eisenhower, went on to surpass his own fame.

Over the past decade and a half, Jack Welch has rightly been held out as an example of a model CEO. Often forgotten in Welch's rise to greatness is the role Reginald Jones, Welch's boss and the former CEO of GE, played in his ascension to power. Jones selected Welch over a number of other, more senior GE executives lined up to replace him. Welch's selection was perhaps even more significant because of how different Welch's style was from that of Jones. However, Jones recognized the environment was changing—just as Marshall recognized the Second World War was going to be far different from the First World War—and he promoted the person he felt had the best set of skills to deal with the future.

"We, in headquarters, live and have our being in order that the people in the field may carry out their mission. If they ask for anything, regardless of its nature, give it to them. If I find out later that their judgment was faulty I will handle the situation." Marshall always made it a habit to free up his subordinates to focus on the task at hand, once saying: "Concentrate on [the] battle with the feeling that it is our business to support you and not harass you and that I'll use all my influence to see that you are supported." Moreover, he did not bother his field officers with little issues and regularly fought bureaucratic battles on their behalf.

Mark Hurd, now CEO of NCR Corp., recounted a story from his second day on the job at NCR in the early 1980s. He had returned from his first sales call with an order, only to be told by a person in the processing department that he had "the wrong form." Hurd told the story to his manager who, in turn, promptly went to the person who said Hurd's order couldn't be processed and declared, "Any time my man comes down here, you are to jump out of your seat and shake his hand because he is keeping you employed. If there is anything wrong with the order you fix it!" Hurd's manager, like Marshall, understood that the headquarters office was there to support the people in the field—and not vice versa.[6]

Dan Cathy, president and COO of Chick-fil-A, Inc., spends at least one day each year working behind the counter of one of his 1,160 fast-food stores; furthermore, he has mandated that the company's other 500 corporate employees do the same thing. Cathy does it because it serves as a reminder to employees at headquarters that they are there to serve their customers and, indirectly, the company's field staff—and not the other way around.[7]

"Pick the right man for the job." George Marshall restructured the army's promotion system because he wanted to be able to put his finger on the person he wanted. He understood that having the right person at the right job was critical to the army's success. Kurt Swogger, head of research and development within a unit of Dow Chemical, has a similar philosophy. When he started at Dow back in the early 1990s, Swogger immediately began asking his employees a series of questions to determine if they were in the right job. What he found startled him. In 1991, only 29 percent of his workforce was in the right job. By 1998, after implementing a more sophisticated system (employing a model based on the Myers-Briggs Type Indicator personality test), Swogger increased that figure to 75 percent. By 2001, he had increased it to 93 percent. During the same period, his team reduced the time it took to launch a new product from between six to fifteen years down to two to four years.[8] Like Marshall, Swogger understood that if the right people were put in the right job at the right time, the right results would follow.

"Let nothing stand in the way of procuring the leadership of the quality necessary." Marshall did more than just say this, he acted on

it. If he had to fire old friends, he did it. If he had to promote junior officers over more senior officers, he did it. If he needed to restructure the U.S. Army's promotion system to get the right people, he got it done. If he needed Congress to pass legislation to give him the freedom to get the right people, he did it. Nothing stood in his way.

Lee Iacocca successfully turned around Chrysler Corporation in part because he had successfully tracked the careers of scores of promising young executives while he was at Ford, and when he was promoted to CEO of Chrysler he brought them over to his new company. (Iacocca actually did have a "little black book" in which he kept the names of quality employees.)

Larry Bossidy, former CEO of Honeywell captured this same sentiment when he wrote, "At the end of the day, you bet on people, not strategies," and his track record suggests that he has done exactly that. Former subordinates of Bossidy include the following CEOs: Paul Norris (W. R. Grace), Dan Burnham (Raytheon), Greg Summe (PerkinElmer), and Frederic Poses (American Standard Companies).[9]

Bill Weiss, one-time CEO of Ameritech (now part of SBC Communications), is another example of a leader not afraid to promote junior officers over more senior personnel. In his effort to transform Ameritech in the mid-1990s, Weiss "skipped over the most obvious choices and selected four people lower in the organization." He did so because in addition to being bright and knowledgeable, they were "aggressive enough to take on unexpected challenges."[10]

If people are a company's most important asset—as so many executives and managers like to say—it is vital that they act like

it were true. This means that picking the right people is one job
that no leader can delegate.

"Give them the bare tree, let them supply the leaves." This was George
Marshall's philosophy regarding army officers. Once he had
selected an officer for a task, he trusted the individual to get the
job done. A modern example of an executive who follows this philosophy is John Stollenwerk, the president, CEO, and owner of
Allen-Edmonds Shoe Corporation—one of the few remaining
shoe manufacturers in America. He has said that the key to his
success is finding talented people who share his "commitment to
quality" and then getting "out of the way" to let them do their job.

*"Deliver me from the lazy thinker . . . give me someone who can and
will think for himself."* As noted earlier, Marshall loved individuals who demonstrated initiative and, even more important,
showed a flair for independent thinking. Larry Bossidy employs
a similar approach. In his book *Execution: The Discipline of
Getting Things Done*, he writes: "You've got to bring in some
other people once in a while to get fresh thoughts, or you're
basically washing yourself in the same dishwasher."[11]

"[M]ake everybody else work like hell." George Marshall lived by
this statement. Once he even declared, "I must have assistants
who will solve their own problems and tell me later what they
have done." Many people have experienced the frustration of
being delegated a particular task by a manager only to have that
manager step in and take over the task before anyone has had a
chance to do anything. In addition to being an inefficient use of

the manager's time, the act also displays a fundamental lack of trust. Both effects are harmful to the overall heath of the organization. Delegation is not a natural reaction for most people, but effective managers understand it is essential and they work at developing the skill.

The Way to Go

In 1952, the day after his protégé Dwight D. Eisenhower was elected president, Marshall scribbled off a quick note congratulating Eisenhower on his victory. He then concluded with this parting advice: "I pray especially for you in the choice of those near to you. That choice, more than anything else, will determine . . . the record of history. Make them meet your standard."

Marshall spoke from experience. He understood that the men and women he had selected, promoted, and supported through his years as chief of staff, secretary of state, and secretary of defense were the ones who wrote his history. And the fact that Eisenhower, his one-time subordinate, went on to surpass him (at least in the eyes of popular culture and modern history) enhances—rather than diminishes—Marshall's reputation as a leader. He understood his primary job was to train, promote, and support other leaders who could carry on and build upon his legacy. More important, Marshall understood that the success of the U.S. Army, and the nation, required that he do no less.

FOCUSING ON THE BIG PICTURE
The Principle of Vision

He was a statesman with a penetrating and commanding view of the whole scene.
—Winston Churchill

He had more mature judgment [and] could see further into the future.
—General Hap Arnold

I never haggled with the president. I swallowed the little things so that I could go to bat on the big ones.
—George C. Marshall

★　★　★　★　★

George Marshall's first recollection as a child occurred when he climbed up the ladder of the family barn in Uniontown, Pennsylvania. As he came to a windowless opening "it seemed a whole world exposed in an instant to my eye." The scene is a fitting visual metaphor for Marshall's eighth leadership principle—the principle of vision—because it accurately captures Marshall's lifelong ability to see the big picture. It was a skill that allowed him to transcend his upbringing in a small frontier constabulary at the beginning of the twentieth century—when the radio, automobile, or airplane were not even invented yet—and emerge into a global statesman charged with administering vast responsibilities on behalf of the most powerful country in the world.

Avoiding Trivia: A History of Focusing on the Big Picture
In August 1913, Marshall reported for his second tour of duty in the Philippines. This time he was assigned to the Thirteenth

Infantry at Fort McKinley. Still only a lieutenant, Marshall had become frustrated with the lack of innovative and strategic thinking in army training and tactics. One day, he made a bet with another officer that the next senior officer to inspect his company would find three minor errors—which he had purposely built into the exercise—while missing three much more serious errors that he had also included.

Marshall won the bet when the inspecting officer documented one soldier who had not shaven, another without a bayonet on his rifle, and a third with an unbuttoned uniform, while missing every one of the more significant errors—including one that exposed Marshall's unit to unnecessary hostile fire. Even more important than winning the bet, Marshall made his point—the purpose of inspections was not to catch small problems, it was to better prepare troops for actual combat.

On the subject of planning for the massive Meuse-Argonne offensive of World War I, Marshall once quipped that when dealing with the allies, "It was [his] fixed policy to make every concession" because it "usually resulted in settling the more important matters to our advantage." He expressed a similar philosophy when he later had to deal with President Franklin D. Roosevelt as chief of staff: "I never haggled with the president. I swallowed the little things so that I could go to bat on the big ones."

In the summer of 1941, Marshall again demonstrated his ability to keep an eye on the big picture as he struggled to convince Congress to extend the service time limitation and keep soldiers in the U.S. Army for an indefinite period. He accepted a number of minor amendments to the bill in order win over a few opponents. Marshall realized the first objective was simply to get Congress to pass the extension (which it did by a single vote); then he could deal with modifying it later. As history proved, Marshall took the right path. After the attack on Pearl Harbor, America was indebted to Marshall's ability "to swallow the little things" because the draftees and National Guardsmen were still in the army and able to mobilize for war quickly.

Marshall's ability to focus on the big picture was best captured in a phrase he articulated to George Kennan. Marshall was secretary of state and had just promoted Kennan to head up the long-range planning staff in the State Department. His instructions to Kennan were short and succinct: "Avoid trivia." It was Marshall's way of telling Kennan to focus on what was important. Kennan responded by conceiving the basis of the containment strategy, which posited that the best way to prevent the spread of communism was to actively resist it everywhere.

What Should Be Done?

In 1940, America was straining to prepare for war. After a particularly tough day in which he had to tell many people things they didn't necessarily want to hear, Marshall commented to a colleague: "If I lose this job, perhaps I can get in a six-ball juggling act." The reference to a juggling act was not far-fetched. At the time, Marshall was responsible for training and reorganizing the army, keeping the president and Congress informed of his activities, maintaining cordial relations with the navy, and keeping an eye on developments in both the Soviet Union and Japan.

As was recounted in Chapter Five, Marshall called his staff together and asked them "What should be done?" The first answer was that the army needed to increase its buildup in order to become better prepared. Beyond that, however, the strategic questions only became more significant. Who was the greater threat to America—Germany or Japan? How should the needs of the United States be balanced against the needs of its allies? And how should assets be allocated between the army, navy, and air force?

The first question was the most important because it dictated how the other questions would be answered. After close consultation with his staff, Marshall came to the conclusion that Germany represented the more dangerous threat, because if Germany was allowed to defeat the Soviet Union and Great Britain, it could consolidate its gains and add increased industrial capacity to its war-fighting capability, and increase its ability to wage war against the United States.

The decision proved critical because it helped Marshall balance what Winston Churchill called "the hungry table"—an offhand reference to the number of nations clamoring for American resources. The Soviet Union, Latin America, and China (in addition to Great Britain) were all demanding U.S. supplies. The decision to focus on Germany meant often saying "no" to Latin America and China and "yes" to Great Britain and the Soviet Union. In short, the answer determined *where* America was going to focus its efforts.

After determining the primary target, Marshall next focused on *who* was going to defeat Germany. Marshall started with a strong belief that Germany could only be defeated through a coordinated effort on behalf of all the allies. Therefore, before the United

States even entered the war, he began to press for the concept of unified command, stating that "[i]f we can make a plan for unified command now, it will solve nine-tenths of our troubles [later]." No local commander, no matter how skilled or competent, Marshall believed, could comprehend the whole situation in a given theater of war. Vital questions concerning the allocations of resources needed to be under the purview of a single commander. The problem, as Marshall was all too aware, was that commanders often paid their first allegiance to their parochial service—be it the army, navy, or air force. Slowly, over time, Marshall wore down his opponents within the U.S. Army and the Navy who were opposed to the idea by reminding them that the costs of unified command were "much less than the hazards." The British remained his fiercest opponents, but he was finally able to persuade them by demonstrating that he was so committed to the idea that he was even willing to select a British commander, General Archibald Percival Wavell, to command the first-ever unified command, the American-British-Dutch-Australian (ABDA) forces in the southwest Pacific theater.

The concept later proved so successful that some historians have claimed it was the second most strategic concept of war (after the Germany-first strategy). It gave the Allied forces a decided advantage over Germany, which lacked a similar policy with Japan and Italy. Marshall claimed that Germany "always planned on a split of the allies . . . [t]hey never for one moment calculated that the allies could continue to conduct combined operations with complete understanding and good faith." And Churchill later added, "Our greatest triumph [lay] in the fact that we achieved the impossible, Allied military unity of command."[1]

Having addressed the issue of "who," Marshall next turned his attention to the question of *how* Germany was going to be defeated. As late as 1943, Great Britain continued to believe the Nazis could be defeated through a combination of peripheral attacks, air power, naval blockades, and propaganda. Marshall insisted that while all were useful, it was only through a massive and sustained land attack that America and her allies could prevail. He said that "[i]t should be recognized as an almost invariable rule that only land armies finally win wars."

It was a hard sell. As one commentator later said, Marshall was "fighting the ghost of the Somme"—the battlefield where the British lost 60,000 soldiers in a single day to German forces in the First World War. Through eleven different conferences in 1942 and 1943, Marshall persevered. First, he convinced Roosevelt of the necessity. As Forrest Pogue wrote, "Marshall was at the president's elbow" constantly reminding him of the need to attack Germany head-on. And Marshall himself later said, "My job was to hold the president down to what we were doing." It was a difficult task because his chief adversary was Winston Churchill, who had the president's ear and was constantly trying to redirect Allied military power to areas that the United States considered peripheral.

Eventually, Marshall triumphed, and after the war he said, "I doubt if I did anything better in the war than keep Churchill on the main point." Even Churchill said of Marshall's efforts during this period that he came to appreciate Marshall's arguments and his reasoning, stating that "he was a statesman with a penetrating and commanding view of the whole scene."

Answering this question then dictated *which* assets received priority consideration and how those assets were to be allocated among the army, navy, and air corps. One of the more critical examples of Marshall's efforts to prioritize resources occurred when he was able to convince Admiral Ernest King, chief of naval operations, that the navy needed to devote more material effort to the production of landing craft (which were required to carry the army troops necessary to defeat the German army) at the expense of battleships—which King and the U.S. Navy wanted to wage war in the Pacific. After the war, Admiral Harold Stark expressed his gratitude by saying, "I simply thank God for you from the bottom of my heart. I don't know how we could have gotten along without you." It was a tribute to Marshall's ability to get everyone to focus on the big picture.

Preventing "Localitis"

Marshall distinguished himself from his theater commanders— most notably Dwight Eisenhower and Douglas MacArthur—in his ability to think in global terms and prioritize resources. In late 1942, the war in the Pacific—particularly in the area around New Guinea and the Solomon Islands—was not going well. In fact, the situation was so bleak that MacArthur at one point declared that "the entire resources of the United States be diverted temporarily to meet the critical situation." It was a classic case of what Marshall termed "localitis." The term was once defined by Marshall's colleague, Hap Arnold, as "a disease theater commanders contract . . . after they have been with their new command for a short time." More succinctly, Marshall used the term to describe commanders who were unable to place their local needs in the proper context of the overall war effort. Invariably, each theater commander felt their theater was being overlooked in terms of its importance and the amount of resources it was receiving.

In the case of MacArthur, the diagnosis fit nicely. He could not comprehend how the situation in North Africa—and specifically how it related to the strategic priority of defeating Germany—was more pressing than his dire situation in the Pacific. It therefore fell to Marshall to explain to MacArthur why the "entire resources" of the nation couldn't be temporarily diverted to his theater.

MacArthur, however, was far from alone in his demands on military resources. Marshall had to inform the U.S. Navy and Chinese leader Chiang Kai-shek why they would have to do with less in their respective fights in the Pacific and in China. And in early 1944, prior to D-Day, when Marshall feared Eisenhower was listening too closely to his British colleagues—who were urging that the impending invasion be postponed in order to take advantage of a new opportunity in the Mediterranean—Marshall sent his protégé a gentle inquiry stating: "I merely wish to be certain that localitis is not developing." Eisenhower understood the message and refused to delay the D-Day invasion to pursue an opportunity of limited advantage in an area of secondary importance. The job, as Marshall constantly reminded everyone, was to win the war as quickly and efficiently as possible, and that could only be done by focusing on strategic priorities.

The Great Decisions

In 1942, Leslie Groves, the officer appointed to oversee the "Manhattan Project" (i.e., the atomic bomb project) came to visit Marshall to request another $100 million for the project. Marshall, after listening to Grove's rationale, approved the request. As Groves departed the office, Marshall said, "It may interest you to know what I was doing. I was writing a check for three dollars and fifty-two cents for grass seed for my lawn."

It is a small moment, in the middle of an average day for Marshall, but the juxtaposition of the two responsibilities nicely captures Marshall's ability to focus on the mundane and the complex. As Dean Acheson later said, Marshall had a "mastery of precise information" and the ability to apprehend "imponderables."

Two historic decisions demonstrate his extraordinary skill in this regard. The first centers on President Truman's decision to use the atomic bomb. Truman assumed office having no knowledge of the weapon. And yet, within three months of learning of its existence, he was told that it would work, and only weeks later he made the decision to employ the bomb. It was a lot of information to absorb in a short period of time, but there to help him through the monumental task was George C. Marshall.

A number of factors weighed in Marshall's advice to the president. First, he had reviewed all of the alternatives. Marshall rejected the air force's belief that Japan could succumb to conventional strategic bombing. He noted that the bombing of Tokyo had killed more than 100,000 citizens and knew that it had no material effect on dampening Japan's resolve to wage war. He also doubted the navy's claim that Japan could be brought to her knees through a naval blockade. Furthermore, he was extremely sensitive to Japan's penchant for fighting to the death. In the battles for Iwo Jima and Okinawa, the United States had suffered 26,000 and 75,000 casualties, respectively, and Marshall understood that an assault on mainland Japan would be substantially more difficult—and costly.

Thus, when informed on July 16, 1945 that the first test bomb had successfully detonated in the New Mexico desert, Marshall counseled the new president to use it. After considering all of the scenarios, he concluded that the bomb had the best potential to save American lives and win the war. Or, as he later said, "[t]he bomb stopped the war. Therefore, it was justifiable."

Such talk may seem uncharacteristically harsh today, but Marshall had pondered the "imponderables" and rendered his advice. In the final analysis, it is hard to imagine Marshall doing anything else. He had two goals: one, win the war, and two, do it as quickly and efficiently as possible. The bomb helped advance both goals.

Marshall again demonstrated his ability to focus on all aspects of an issue when proposing the Marshall Plan. It has been called by some historians and political commentators "the greatest decision in our history," and while such a statement may sound like hyperbole today, in 1947 Europe was teetering dangerously close to collapse and the Soviet Union stood poised to rush into the breach. To a fair degree, as Marshall said, the "survival of the kind of world in which democracy, individual liberty, economic stability, and peace can be maintained" rested on its success.

Because Marshall's mind, as Dean Acheson said, did not work merely along military lines, he was able to focus on finding the most constructive solution to the problem—which, in this instance, was an economic solution. Moreover, Marshall realized that to be successful two things were essential. First, the initiative could not be an American-led effort. It had to be led by the participating European nations and, as such, they had to develop their own unified list of priorities and action items. Second, the economic resources the United States committed could not be used to meet short-term needs. The aid had to be devoted to building up the industrial infrastructure of the war-torn nations. And it was these two requirements that got the nations of Europe to work together and concentrate their collective efforts on creating the conditions that ultimately fostered long-term growth, stability, and prosperity on the continent.

It is a tribute to Marshall's ability to focus on what was really important during the chaotic and critical days of 1947 that allowed Europe to employ the tools to pursue this peaceful and prosperous path.

Lessons: In His Own Words

"What do we think should be done?" This was the question that Marshall asked his staff before the beginning of World War II. And it was on the basis of this question that he felt compelled to begin educating President Roosevelt about the "true strategic picture of what faced the United States." By continuously asking the question, Marshall was also able to achieve "unity of command" and develop the "Germany first" approach—the two most important strategic concepts of the war.

In a 2004 article for the *Harvard Business Review,* management and leadership expert Peter Drucker reminded his readers that the first question any executive must ask herself is: What needs to be done? Drucker then went on to say executives must have the courage to change direction if presented with new information. The example Drucker cited was Marshall's peer, President Harry Truman. When Truman became president, he was primarily interested in issues of economic and social justice. America's victory in the war, however, changed everything, and Truman understood that it was his responsibility to focus his efforts and those of the nation on issues of international peace and stability.[2]

A business example can be found in the actions of Andy Grove when he was CEO of Intel Corporation. In the 1970s, Intel had a strong and growing business in the field of semiconductors, especially memory chips. By the mid-1980s, Japanese competition had pushed Intel to the brink of a crisis. Grove then had a candid conversation with the company founder, Gordon Moore, and they decided that given the strength of the new competition, if they were to succeed as a company they had to get out of their biggest business and begin anew in the field of microprocessors. And that is exactly what they did.

The retail chain Toys "R" Us, offers a more recent example. Throughout the 1980s and well into the 1990s, the retailer's strategy of providing a wide selection of high-quality toys at reasonable prices proved very successful. Once Wal-Mart entered the market, however, annual double-digit growth stopped for Toys "R" Us. To its credit, the company has deemphasized the sales of children's toys and moved quickly into the baby supply and equipment market. It is entirely possible—indeed, likely— that Wal-Mart and others will also follow Toys "R" Us into this market, but the aggressive approach has, at a minimum, bought the company a few more years of high growth.

"I merely wish to be certain that localitis is not developing and that pressures on you have not warped your judgment." This was Marshall's response to Eisenhower when he feared his protégé was being

unduly influenced by those around him to pursue an alternative that was not in the strategic interests of the United States.

Having served in the cabinet of Minnesota Governor Jesse Ventura, I personally witnessed "localitis" on a number of occasions. Commissioners of state agencies, especially if they are newly appointed, are often forced to rely on the assistance and advice of career civil servants when approaching the state legislature for their annual funding. The civil servants—whose self-interest lies in enlarging the size and influence of their own department—frequently encourage and convince the new commissioners to request more than the governor (who has a responsibility to the entire state) deems appropriate. Sadly, many commissioners develop "localitis" and become advocates for only their agency—with no regard to the overall strategic picture.

A good executive quickly puts an end to this silo-type thinking either by reminding people of the big picture or, if necessary, relieving them of their jobs if they are unable to subvert their agency's parochial interests to the strategic goals of the entire organization.

"We must not jeopardize our sound overall strategy to exploit local success in a generally accepted secondary theater." In 1943, the British hoped to exploit Allied success in Italy by attacking the northern Balkans. Marshall refused. He knew the quickest way to defeat Germany was by attacking the Nazis head-on, and he was not about to have troops, material, or equipment siphoned off to gain a dubious advantage in a secondary theater of operation.

Jack Welch adhered to a similar philosophy while CEO of GE. Shortly after assuming the top spot, he told the company divisions that they were either going to be first or second in their respective fields—or GE was going to get out of the business. By adhering to this strategy, Welch was able to increase GE's market capitalization by $450 billion in twenty years.

"Avoid trivia." This was Marshall's famous advice to George Kennan when he asked him to outline a plan of action for dealing with the Soviet Union in the early years of the Cold War. A more mundane application of these two words occurred many years earlier, in France in World War I. Marshall went to visit some American soldiers who had been wounded in a surprise raid. Upon entering the triage center he found a sergeant typing out lengthy reports on the condition of each soldier instead of helping to treat them. "What the hell are you going to do if you have a battle with a thousand casualties?" Marshall asked. The sergeant put up some resistance, but Marshall ordered him to drop the report and "get to work on these men." He understood that the work on the report was "trivia."

Peter Drucker has a comparable saying: "First things first, second things not at all." The implied message is that executives cannot afford to allow their subordinates or organizations to become preoccupied with inconsequential matters. The job of leaders is to first focus their own time, attention, and energy on the most important aspect of the business, and then channel and redirect the energy of the entire organization toward the same end.

"Face up to our vast responsibility." Marshall offered this blunt assessment to the American people when he proposed the Marshall Plan. He knew the nation was tired after four years of

fighting and most American's desperately wanted to return to their normal lives. He also understood the war's victory had thrust extraordinary new responsibility on the country. As a leader, it was his job to make the public face up to those responsibilities.

Again, Peter Drucker acknowledges the same point when he says that the first question any good leader asks is: "What is the foremost need of the institution—and therefore my first task?"

In 1997, Xerox Corporation brought in Richard Thoman to make changes. In his overzealousness, he attempted to make two very significant changes at the same time. One required consolidating the company's ninety administrative centers; the second called for switching the sales force's emphasis from a geographical focus to an industry focus. Both decisions were important, but the consolidation of the centers needed to be Thoman's first priority because it would have immediately reduced costs and improved efficiency. Attempting to do both things simultaneously resulted in chaos, and Thoman was fired in early 2000.

Now compare Thoman's actions with those of Gordon Bethune when he took over Continental Airlines in 1994 and it was ranked dead last among the top-ten major airlines. By focusing on on-time takeoffs and addressing customer complaints, Bethune was able within one year to move up to first place in the J. D. Power's report of customer satisfaction. Then, after achieving that goal, he was able to devote his attention to creating an incentive program for the aircrew and begin rebuilding relationships with corporate customers and travel agents. In short, Bethune didn't try to do everything his first year—he just focused on the most important job.

During the war—and contrary to the opinions of the navy as well as most Americans who favored a Japan-first policy— Marshall understood Germany had to be defeated first and therefore resources had to be allocated accordingly. An attempt to wage war against Germany and Japan by splitting the resources equally would have likely prolonged the war and, quite possibly, jeopardized success.

"Go home and think about it." In 1948, an aide suggested to Marshall that the United States might employ an atomic bomb to resolve the Berlin blockade. Marshall asked the aide if he would bomb Leningrad and the Hermitage—the famous Russian museum—in the heart of the city. The aide conceded he might spare the Hermitage. Marshall then said that if he were serious, why was there even a question. He then told the aide to "go home and think about it." Marshall refused to accept the allure of easy answers and always thought through the long-term consequences of his decisions.

"It takes more skills and knowledge to cut red tape than any other particular endeavor I know in government." Early in 1917, Marshall became aware that soldiers preparing to go to war in Europe did not have blankets, mattresses, and other essential supplies. When he encountered a supply officer who challenged his authority to ship in those supplies at great expense, Marshall replied, "The cost was not going to mean so much to those men freezing up there." He then reminded the officer of the bad publicity the army would receive if news of such poor treatment was released to the public. Marshall refused to allow bureaucrats—

who often had a narrow perspective on a problem—to stop him from focusing on what was truly important.

The job of any manager, executive, or leader is to do the same thing. And they must understand that while rules are put in place for a variety of legitimate and worthwhile reasons, circumstances vary and it is the leader's job to see to it that overly bureaucratic rules are not allowed to prevent activities or stifle initiatives that are in the strategic interest of the organization.

Bruce Burlington, the former head of the Food and Drug Administration's Center for Devices and Radiological Health (CDRH) unit, was responsible for the FDA's approval of such lifesaving medical devices as pacemakers. For years, Congress flatlined his budget, which had the indirect affect of slowing the approval process. Realizing that lives were at stake, Burlington responded by directing that low-risk medical devices be dropped from CDRH's close scrutiny, thereby allowing more time and attention to be directed toward the truly critical devices.[3]

"War in a democracy is no bed of roses." This was Marshall's response when asked how he reacted to having to address political issues when his primary job (at least during World War II) was military in nature. In the fall of 1942 (when Marshall offered this quote), he was forced to concede that it was important to attack Germany in North Africa—as opposed to delaying the fight until America was better prepared to wage the much bigger fight on the continent—because President Roosevelt needed to be seen as doing something for external political reasons.

Many business leaders today can appreciate the conflict Marshall must have felt as he struggled to juggle both military and political issues. It is comparable to saying shareholders, employees, *and* a commitment to long-term growth all come first. Clearly, trade-offs have to be made. It's a juggling act, and the trick is to keep the smaller balls (e.g., shareholders and employees) in the air while never taking an eye off long-term growth. For in the end, if long-term growth isn't achieved, neither the shareholders, the employees, nor the business itself will prosper.

"If we can make a plan for unified command now, it will solve nine-tenths of our troubles." Marshall offered this quote when the allies needed to act as a single unit. His underlining motivation was a strong desire to get all the allies focused on the most strategic goal—defeating Germany. The same thinking prompted him to reorganize the War Department during the early part of World War II and reduce the number of people who reported directly to him from sixty to six. Marshall understood that organizational change was often essential if the institution wanted to focus on priorities.

When Dick Brown became the CEO of Electronic Data Systems (EDS) in 1999 (a position he held until 2003), he found that there were more than forty strategic business units organized across a variety of different fields. He successfully reorganized the units into four distinct lines of business and freed himself up to concentrate on strategic issues, such as improving communication within the company, developing a compensation system that rewarded performers, and focusing his energies on whichever line of business he felt required his time.[4]

The Way to Go

A week before George Marshall accepted the position of secretary of defense in 1950, General Douglas MacArthur implemented a bold and daring amphibious landing at the port of Inchon, near Seoul, South Korea. The surprise attack literally turned the tide of the Korean War, and American and South Korean forces rushed across the thirty-eighth parallel to press their advantage. Victory appeared within reach, but as the United Nations forces approached the Yalu River (and the border with China), the Chinese counterattacked in force and swiftly and dramatically changed the entire context of the war.

By late November 1950, MacArthur was warning that the United States was facing "an entirely new war" and advocated a massive counterattack into China. President Truman and George Marshall felt such an act might bring the Soviet Union into the fight—something they strongly wished to avoid. As a result, the Truman administration began to pursue a strategy that focused on achieving a cease-fire.

MacArthur disagreed with the approach and made public statements to that effect. In December, Truman ordered MacArthur to desist from making any further public statements without first clearing them with Washington.

The tension between Truman and MacArthur continued to simmer in the early months of 1951 until, in early April, a prominent Republican leader read a letter from MacArthur criticizing Truman's approach to the war.

The president asked Marshall for his advice on how to handle the situation. After much deliberation, Marshall concluded that MacArthur should be relieved of his duty.

Marshall understood that there was more at issue than a simple case of disobedience. The first was that MacArthur was suffering from "localitis." As Omar Bradley later said during a hearing into MacArthur's dismissal, his strategy of attacking China would have gotten America "into the wrong war, at the wrong place, at the wrong time, and with the wrong enemy." In essence, Marshall realized that MacArthur couldn't comprehend the big picture and didn't fully appreciate how Europe and, specifically, the growing threat from the Soviet Union, factored into America's strategic interests.

Even more important than this fact, in Marshall's mind, however, was the simple fact that MacArthur was guilty of insubordination. In a democracy, the military—and its leaders—must be subservient to its civilian leaders. It was not a principle that could be bent to fit the whims of a particular personality—no matter how popular that figure may be. The reason, as Marshall well understood, was because in a democracy, civilian leadership is charged with considering all sides of an issue—political, economic, and military—and then focusing the nation's attention, resources, and energy toward a set of policies designed to achieve a strategic vision.

At the time, *Time* magazine wrote, "Never has a less popular figure fired a more popular one." Yet Truman (who ultimately made and took responsibility for the decision) realized, like Marshall, that focusing on what is truly important isn't always popular—but it is necessary for ensuring the integrity and long-term success of any organization.

N E

SUPPORTING
THE TROOPS
The Principle of Caring

The combat soldier never had a better or more understanding friend than George C. Marshall.
—General Matthew Ridgway

We will take care of the troops first, last, and all of the time.
—George C. Marshall

⋆ ⋆ ⋆ ⋆ ⋆

In 1940, Marshall, in his quest to rid the U.S. Army Officer Corps of "poor fish," fired a number of National Guard generals who owed their positions more to political patronage than military skill. One particular general refused to accept the harsh verdict and lobbied his home state's entire congressional delegation to force Marshall to reconsider his decision. Marshall refused and informed the congressmen that if pressed, he would resign. "I'll put it this way, gentlemen," he went to say, "I don't understand your position because I should think your constituents should be your principal interest—and here it seems to me that you are only considering one constituent and ignoring all [your] other constituents who are members of the division. I am concerned with them . . ."[1]

Later that evening, after the politicians backed down, one of the senators recounted the story for his wife. She then reminded her husband that their own son was in the division and she, for one, was thrilled that Marshall was looking out for their son's best interests as opposed to the general's. Marshall's willingness to protect and support his troops first lies at the heart of Marshall's ninth leadership principle—the principle of caring.

A History of Caring for the Troops

In 1904, Marshall was stationed in Fort Reno—then just part of the territory of Oklahoma. The area surrounding the military base was in awful condition. Homes were rundown, unpainted, and bug-infested, and the neighborhood yards were unkempt and filled with litter. Marshall set about rectifying the situation immediately because he could see the negative effect it was having on morale. (In fact, Marshall would later claim that a good officer could instantly assess the morale of the soldiers at any given post merely by looking at the condition of the surrounding facilities.) In this instance, he was hampered by a lack of funds, but he refused to let that stop him. One day an army wife approached him with a request that he do something to fix her kitchen. Marshall replied that he would help her on the condition that she first "fix up her yard." The woman eagerly consented.

A few weeks later, impressed at what she had accomplished, Marshall ordered that the necessary supplies be found and the woman's kitchen painted. Soon, the other neighborhood women began asking for similar treatment, and within a matter of a week the entire base underwent a marked physical transformation and, along with it, a noticeable improvement in morale.

Later, while serving in Arkansas, Marshall again demonstrated his concern for his troops—only this time he directed his attention to their children. Shortly before Christmas, Marshall learned that no festivities were planned. On his own initiative, he began collecting money from the other officers. Then he convinced local merchants to donate gifts and secured the services of Santa Claus to organize a Christmas party. He even put the army prisoners to work fixing up the gymnasium where the party would be held.

The event was a huge success, and afterward a man speaking on behalf all the prisoners thanked Marshall for everything he had done for the children and their families. The party was, he added, the first Christmas that most of the prisoners had ever had, so he told Marshall that if there was ever anything the prisoners could do to help him in the future, all he needed to do was ask.

Marshall always felt that wars would be won by the side that convinced their soldiers to "do the impossible." But before they could rise to that level, he believed that the troops had to know their officers always had their best interests at heart. In small ways and in out-of-the-way commands—either by painting their houses or throwing holiday parties—Marshall demonstrated that concern.

At Fort Benning, during the Depression, Marshall instituted a policy of providing the enlisted men—whose wages hovered near subsistence level—the opportunity to buy a hot meal for their families for a dime. When he was with the Fifteenth Regiment in China, he arranged weekly sporting competitions, built skating rinks, arranged hunts, and even organized theatrical productions.[2] During his time overseeing civilians members of the Civilian Conservation Corps (CCC), Marshall employed dentists to fix their teeth and engaged tutors and teachers to help them learn to read and write. He even wrote letters of recommendations on their behalf to help them gain employment in the private sector after they had completed their duty.

And when he became the army's top-ranking officer in 1939, Marshall signaled how much he valued morale by making the Office of the Army Morale its own special branch and recruiting one of America's leading CEOs at the time, Frederick Osborn, to run the department. Shortly into his term, he even traveled to a small southern military town to assess the situation of his troops. Wearing only civilian clothes, Marshall walked around the town and was distressed at what he found. Soldiers had to wait for hours to get a warmed-over meal, and often there were no planned recreational activities. Because there were no organized events to raise the morale and address the social needs of the soldiers, he recognized it was only a matter of time before there was serious trouble. So, when he returned to Washington, Marshall took the first step toward organizing what would later become known as the United Services Organization—or the USO.

Upon entry into war, Marshall continued his commitment to the USO by ensuring that many of the day's top entertainers, including Bob Hope, Bing Crosby, Fred Astaire, Marlene Dietrich, and Dinah Shore, participated in the organization. He also sent Irving Berlin's "This Is the Army" show all over the world.

First, Last, and All the Time

On a daily basis, throughout the war, Marshall made it a point to read a summary of soldiers' complaints and respond to a minimum of six letters every day. He created roving "ambassadors" to visit the troops and learn of—and rectify—problems. As a result of his efforts, recreational facilities were set up and shoes and uniforms were modified for comfort. Once, upon learning that a request for extra blankets had gone unaddressed, Marshall was furious and called in the members of the quartermaster staff. When offered an explanation, Marshall exploded, saying, "I want the matter resolved now." He concluded his short lecture by saying, "We are going to take care of the troops first, last, and all the time."[3]

An equally famous story has Marshall admonishing his supply staff after learning during one of his many inspections that some of the troops in the field were short of uniforms. When he pressed his staff, Marshall was shown lists proving that their warehouses were stacked. Unimpressed with mere paperwork, he ordered the department to act as though it was a mail-order company trying to dispose of surplus stock. To make sure his point was not lost, he announced to everyone within earshot, "I am interested in the soldier having his pants!"

He was passionate about these things because, as he once said, "Our soldiers must be keenly conscious that the full strength of our nation is behind them . . . we [must] never forget for a moment that the soldier has been compelled to leave his family, to give up his business, and to hazard his life in our service."

And Marshall acted on this belief. After meeting a survivor of the Bataan Death March of 1942, he ordered his personal plane to transport the man around the country so he could be reunited with his extended family. When he learned that the first group of army WAC nurses sent to North Africa in 1942 had lost all of their personal belongings when their ship was torpedoed, he obtained replacement clothing for them—at his own personal expense.

After the war, Marshall continued to demonstrate uncommon compassion for his troops. He accepted the presidency of the Red Cross, in part, because of his concern for the well-being of the hundreds of thousands of troops who were still in need of help because of the physical and mental wounds they suffered during the war.

Even in his retirement, Marshall could not help but look after the morale and welfare of his troops and their families. A soldier once wrote him at his retirement cottage in Pinehurst, North Carolina, and explained that he had been unfairly stationed in Japan instead of near his wife—as he was promised when he agreed to reenlist. Marshall, on his own initiative, investigated the matter and then took the time to drive to visit the soldier's wife and explain the situation. Eight days later, the man was reunited with his wife and family. Marshall was true to his word—he had taken care of his troops first, last, and all the time.

Listening, Rewarding, and Doing the Little Things

Not long after the Second World War began, Marshall was approached by the famous pollster Elmer Roper, who convinced him of the need to use modern polling to determine the likes and dislikes of the soldiers. Marshall readily agreed. He did so not because of a need or a desire to be popular—as many of today's political leaders use the polling technique—but rather because he was convinced that citizen-soldiers with grievances that went unaddressed later became civilian opponents of the army. Moreover, as Forrest Pogue wrote, Marshall's willingness to listen to the complaints of the newest recruit and correct them "was the essence of democracy" and that "was what the fighting was all about."[4]

Once Marshall was making an inspection of Fort Knox and as he worked his way through the first few rows of soldiers, he stopped and spoke with one soldier. He was later asked why he stopped and Marshall replied, "I caught the man's eye and I knew something was wrong. I wanted to find out what." It took him a few minutes to get at the heart of the matter, but eventually Marshall learned that the draft board had made a serious mistake in drafting the man. He was overage, in poor physical condition, and had a large family to support.[5] By the end of the day, because of Marshall's intervention, the man was discharged and sent back to his family.

After the war, Marshall elaborated on his alleged soft treatment of his troops. "As to coddling the soldiers, I was responsible for as much of that abroad as anybody because I felt we had to do everything we could to make the men feel that we had the highest solicitude for their condition . . . . They were being taken from home; they were being taken away from [work] and their wives and families . . . I was for supplying everything we could and then requiring him to fight to the death when the time came. You had to put these two things together," he added, because "[i]f it were all solicitude, then you had no army. But you couldn't be severe in your demands unless [the soldier] was convinced that you were doing everything you could to make matters well for him . . . ."

And Marshall did almost everything humanly possible to make matters well. He reorganized the army's post exchange service and ordered that in combat zones no exchanges be allowed to open on supply bases until the front lines had first received similar service. He worked hard to ensure the troops were supplied with Hershey Bars, Coca-Cola, and cigarettes and, to the extent possible, that they had turkey, cranberries, and dressing on Thanksgiving and Christmas.

"Many of our people forget the importance of little things to morale," Marshall once said, and he vowed when he "got to the top that . . . things would be set up quickly along this line, since the men think if there is candy up forward, things can't be so bad."

Marshall's career is filled with stories of him doing hundreds of the small things that, when viewed in aggregate, paint a very flattering picture of a caring and compassionate man. While commander of the Fifth Brigade, Third Division, in Washington State, Marshall was once approached by a sergeant on behalf of a soldier whose son was suffering from polio. The sergeant asked him if he would write a letter so the boy might gain admittance to the Shiners' Hospital. Marshall refused the request, but before the stunned sergeant could protest, Marshall replied that he was going to personally go up to the hospital to rectify the matter.[6]

On another occasion, Marshall learned that a young army officer was trying to get transferred to Hawaii so he could marry a nurse in Pearl Harbor. Unwilling to transfer the man, Marshall did the next best thing and allowed the officer to accompany some classified material that he knew needed to be transported to Pearl Harbor.

Even at the end of the war, Marshall, in a moment of poetic justice, continued to demonstrate that he never forgot the plight of the common soldier. In early November 1945, Henry Stimson officially resigned as secretary of war. Marshall traveled to Andrews Air Force Base to send him off. The day was unusually hot and a group of senior military officers—all generals and admirals—were standing at attention on the hot tarmac. An aide suggested that they be allowed to stand at ease and come in out of the sun. Marshall just smiled and said, "Those officers have kept more GIs waiting in the sun than you and I can count, and it's about time they found out what it's like. By golly, let them wait." And they did, until Marshall finally ordered them to stand at ease.[7]

But Marshall did more than just do the little things. He also made it a priority to reward and recognize people if they had served admirably or performed above and beyond the call of duty. "Men can stand almost anything if their works receive public acknowledgment," he once said. That is why he lobbied President Franklin Roosevelt for the creation of the Bronze Star Medal ("for heroic and meritorious achievement or service . . . against an enemy of the United States"). Marshall also believed in rewarding people quickly, declaring that "[d]ecorations and service ribbons are of real value to the war effort only if promptly bestowed." On numerous occasions Marshall ordered citations drafted immediately for individual commanders or units that displayed meritorious service in combat and then had their names released to the press so they could receive public recognition as well. The paperwork would follow later.

In the case of awarding Douglas MacArthur the Medal of Honor, Marshall even took the lead in writing the citation himself. One of the reasons he cited to Secretary of War Stimson in requesting the award was the "constructive morale value" the medal would have—not only on MacArthur's troops (then under siege in the Philippines) but on the American public, which, at the time, was still reeling from Pearl Harbor and the series of setbacks the United States suffered in the immediate weeks and months following the surprise attack.

Marshall did not limit himself to ribbons and rewards. He continuously fought for higher pay for enlisted personnel. As early as the 1930s, when Congress passed a 15 percent reduction in pay to junior officers, Marshall "prepared a spirited protest" in which he demonstrated that junior officers were making less money in 1932 than they had in 1908. Although he was unsuccessful in getting Congress to reconsider the issue, years later, when he had the ear of President Roosevelt and was in a better position to do something about it, Marshall convinced the president and Congress to provide an additional five dollars monthly pay for each serviceman who earned Expert Infantryman Badge and another five dollars for those earning the Combat Infantryman Badge.

Listening, doing the small things, and rewarding people— all of these actions are central to the leadership principle of caring. Yet the depth of Marshall's commitment to his troops can be found in the simple fact that he never forgot them. Every Christmas, he would send a note to the commander and men in each and every isolated outpost where American troops were stationed. It is a testament to his dedication to his troops that even with his extraordinary responsibilities for managing a global war, he never forgot about the men and women fighting and dying in such remote places as the Aleutians, the Pribilof Islands, the Himalaya Mountains, and Ascension Island. His letters demonstrated that he recognized their sacrifices and was ever cognizant of the contributions his troops were providing to victory.

Marshall's real concern for his troops can, however, best be seen in how he handled the most difficult and painful aspect of his job. Early in the war, he made it a point to write a personal note to the parents of every man killed in action. But as the casualties mounted and the burden became too time-consuming, Marshall still made time for cases where a family lost two or more sons. One such note read:

> I have just learned that your twin sons Carl and Clarence were killed . . . . Please accept my deep sympathies in your overwhelming loss. While few American families have been completely spared from the tragic consequences of this terrible struggle, you have been called upon for a much greater sacrifice than most and I pray that you will find the faith and strength to endure your loss.

Marshall knew from experience what he was talking about because his own stepson, Allen, was killed by a German sniper while fighting in Italy.

Understanding the pain of such losses was one of the reasons why Marshall always presented the casualty reports to President Roosevelt in vivid, color graphics. He did not want his commander-in-chief to become immune to the loss of his troops. He knew that behind every statistic was a real person with a real family, and Marshall was not going to allow himself, his president, or the country to ever forget that fact.

Lessons: In His Own Words

"Morale is primarily a function of command." George Marshall issued this comment upon hearing from a general that the morale of his troops was low. As secretary of state, Marshall also once told his staff: "Gentlemen, it is my experience [that] an enlisted man may have a morale problem. An officer is expected to take care of his own morale."[8] The two statements were his way of saying that the issue of morale cannot be delegated. It starts at the top and if there is a problem, that is the first place a good leader must go to address the issue.

It has been said that "leaders lead." In the case of morale, this is particularly true. If there is a problem, the leader is the one responsible for fixing it. In 1998, Marilyn Carlson Nelson became the CEO of Carlson Companies, a multibillion-dollar, privately held hospitality and services company located in Minnetonka, Minnesota. During a meeting with some MBA students who had been studying the company's corporate culture, she was astounded to learn that the internal impression of her company was that it was "a sweatshop that doesn't care."

Nelson immediately went into action and created "Carlson Cares," a program designed to change the company's culture. Long-time executives at the company urged Nelson to go slow. She refused to take that approach. By interacting with her employees on a daily basis and establishing another program called "Creating a Great Place for Great People to Work," Nelson was able to change the culture. In 2002, her company was named by *Fortune* magazine as one of the "100 Best Companies to Work For" in America.[9]

"We are going to take care of the troops first, last, and all the time." At the end of the day, Marshall understood that it was not going to be him, his generals, or even the officer corps who were going to win the war; it was going to be the troops on the battlefield. And for them to do their best, they had to know their leaders always had their best interest at heart. Therefore, he made it an absolute priority to take care of his troops.

It is almost a cliché for executives to say that "employees are our most important asset." Unfortunately, reality doesn't always match the rhetoric. James Nicholson, President and CEO of PVS Chemicals, for one, has found a way to move beyond rhetoric. He has made the safety of his employees his number-one priority. He personally teaches classes on safety and rewards behavior that improves safety in a number of ways—including the distribution of monetary gifts. His actions back up his claims.[10] Bill George, the former CEO of Medtronic, backed up his rhetoric when he openly expressed to his shareholders that his employees' best interests came before their interests. He understood what numerous studies have demonstrated— employees who are happy and feel respected are more productive and, in turn, make their corporations more profitable.

A classic example of taking care of troops is offered by Ann Hambly, managing director at Prudential Asset Resources. One of her workers once had a family emergency and needed to fly home. At the time, the employee couldn't afford the flight, so Hambly purchased the ticket for him. Her example recalls the story of Marshall buying replacement clothing for the WAC nurses who lost their belongings when their ship was sunk.[11] In neither case did the act represent a huge financial sacrifice; what mattered was that the leader had actively demonstrated their concern.

"When we are tired, cold, and hungry, at the end of the day it is the leader who puts aside his personal discomfort to look to the needs of his soldiers." Marshall's second tour of duty took him to Fort Reno where, among his other responsibilities, he was charged with surveying a large portion of Texas badlands. It was brutal work and required Marshall and his team to endure temperatures as hot as 130 degrees. During one particularly difficult stretch, the team began to run dangerously low on water. They instituted a policy of rationing, but it wasn't enough; it was apparent that their water would run out unless drastic action was taken. As the leader, Marshall instinctively went without water for the final fifty miles in order that his men wouldn't have to suffer thirst. It was a small act in the middle of nowhere, but it vividly displayed that Marshall's first concern was for his troops—not himself.[12]

A modern parallel can be found in the small business owner who, during the early days of starting the business and getting it up and running, forgoes a paycheck while ensuring that her employees get theirs. In fact, that is just what Vicki Henry, CEO of Feedback Plus, a small marketing research firm, did during her first few years when money was extremely tight.

"I am interested in the soldier having his pants." Marshall made this remark after learning that his troops did not have the proper uniforms. Through this comment, Marshall was acknowledging that the soldier's uniform was a constant presence. As such, its look and feel could serve as a positive reminder of the army's treatment and respect for the average soldier, or (if neglected) it could serve as a negative reminder. This same thinking led Marshall, at every post where he ever served, to improve the physical presence. He understood that morale, like pride, has a strong material element. The daily work condition of a company or organization often is a direct reflection on how that company cares for its employees. For instance, if a building is not kept clean or if the parking lot lighting is not maintained, it is only natural that the employees will feel undervalued.

Vera Katz, the mayor of Portland, Oregon, annually sends 10,000 surveys to the citizens of Portland. She asks for ratings on public transportation, the police department, the water bureau, and environmental services. She also seeks more basic information, such as whether the citizens think the streets are clean and safe and whether the quality of the city's parks is being maintained. Katz then benchmarks the results against other cities and shares the results with Portland's residents in a variety of different ways—including hosting a television program to go over the findings.[13]

"Take road trips with no visible signs of rank [to] find out . . . what conditions actually are, and take proper steps for the correction of defects." Marshall always made it a priority to travel and listen to his troops' concerns, as well as their suggestions for improvement. Then,

to demonstrate his commitment, he made it a policy to address at least one of their concerns either by the time he left the post or, if it required more extensive action, no less than a few days after returning to Washington.

David Novak, the chairman and CEO of YUM! Brands, Inc., (which owns KFC, Pizza Hut, and Taco Bell), makes it a point to listen to his employees. In fact, he attributes his success to going out to the front lines and meeting with the salespeople, the people in the warehouses, and the production teams on a regular basis.[14] David Neeleman, CEO of JetBlue Airways, does the same thing when he stays after a flight and helps the crew clean the plane. He uses the time not only to get to know his employees better, but he also listens to find out what is wrong and what is going right with his company's operations. He then takes corrective action to fix the former and reward the latter.

Lou Smith, president and CEO of the Ewing Marion Kauffman Foundation, has publicly stated that listening is the key to his organization's success. In fact, five times a year Smith convenes a group of thirty to fifty associates solely to listen to their ideas, suggestions, and anything else they may want to talk about.[15]

Larry Bossidy, former chairman and CEO of Honeywell, has said that such actions convey to employees that the CEO "cares enough about my business to come and review it." It also raises the dignity of employees by acknowledging their work.

"The men think if there is candy up forward, things can't be so bad." Marshall made it a point to make sure his troops had as many creature comforts as possible. For instance, he did not have to make it a priority that his troops had Hershey Bars, Coca-Cola,

and cigarettes, but he did. In a larger sense, this statement, coupled with his actions, captures Marshall's willingness to do the little things.

Today's leaders can do any number of small things that are well within their purview: They can provide their employees with free coffee and purified water. They can improve the office space by having music, plants, better lighting, and parking on the premises. They can also do some more significant things, too, such as offering on-site day care, flex time, and job sharing. And while all executives must use their own best judgment to determine which "creature comforts" make sense, from both a morale and a business perspective, they should not minimize the importance of doing at least a few of the little things. Often an increase in morale leads directly to increased productivity, which, in turn, more than offsets the minimal price of the perk.

For instance, Genencor International, a biotech company located in Palo Alto, California, has gone to extraordinary lengths to take care of its employees. In 1996, company leaders took the unusual step of allowing employees to have a say in the design of their new building. Their input led to the labs having more natural light sources as well as the construction of a "main street" where employees can congregate, collaborate, and interact throughout the day. Genencor also regularly polls its employees about which benefits they enjoy and which new benefits they would like to see offered. Among the more innovative perks are cars for employees who must rely on public transportation (to use to run errands during the day), and on-site photo processing, dry cleaning, and dental services. The company even offers emergency child-care services.

Genencor estimates that the cost of these services is approximately $700 per employee. However, when one considers the company's annual turnover rate is less than 4 percent (compared with a national average of 18.5 percent), and the cost of recruiting and training a new employee is $75,000, then these services make economic sense. Furthermore, Genencor employees generate $60,000 more revenue per employee than its largest competitor, so the benefits are even more clear.[16]

"Decorations and service ribbons are of real value . . . only if promptly bestowed." Marshall believed that rewards were useless unless they were bestowed quickly. To do otherwise simply lowered morale because it caused people to feel underappreciated and hurt unit effectiveness by making it less likely that a person would give 100 percent to future tasks.

Nancy Hutson is the senior vice president of global research and development at Pfizer. The drug industry is notorious for its high-risk, low-success-rate approach to finding a new drug. Often scientists can spend an entire career without discovering a lifesaving or life-enhancing drug. In such an environment, it is difficult to keep people motivated. Hutson has tackled the issue, in part, by rewarding small victories. If a researcher publishes a paper or if a lab gets a positive result, she is quick to acknowledge the good news throughout the organization. Such small victories, she says, help her team deal more effectively with the reality that a "big victory" may not be just around the corner.[17]

Other examples of quick recognition include Hewlett-Packard's "Golden Banana" award, Walt Disney's "Spirit of Fred" award, and Maritz Performance Improvement Company's

"Thanks a Bunch" program. In each case, the award itself—be it a Golden Banana or a bunch of flowers—is small. What matters is that it is given with sincerity and bestowed promptly.[18]

The Way to Go

At a speech at Trinity College in Hartford, Connecticut, in June of 1941, shortly before the outbreak of war, Marshall said that while it is true that war was fought with the "physical weapons of flame and steel," they did not achieve victory. Instead, he declared, "It is morale that wins the victory. It is steadfastness and courage and hope. It is confidence and zeal and loyalty. It is élan, *esprit de corps*, and determination."

As this chapter has demonstrated, Marshall's entire life spoke to this belief. One story, in particular, however, stands out. It occurred in the middle of the First World War.

A young captain, who was the commander of a machine-gun battalion, had just participated in a vicious battle. The captain's company had expended more than 100,000 rounds of ammunition and four of his guns had been destroyed by artillery fire. When the battle was over, his company was relieved and ordered to return to the rear area. Upon returning, however, the captain learned that his unit was being recalled to the front. Angry over the change in orders—which was made worse because another machine-gun company that hadn't seen any fighting was allowed to stay—he demanded to see the general. Instead, he encountered Colonel Marshall. In a calm voice, Marshall described the importance of holding the region and explained that he had personally selected the officer's company because of its extraordinary skill.

The captain later reflected that an "officer of a different type" would have reacted curtly to his belligerent tone and simply ordered him out of his office and up to the front. The captain instead left the meeting "with a feeling of added pride in my outfit . . . [t]he morale of the officers and men was restored and we went into fighting that night a better unit than we had ever been before."[19] And it was all because Marshall acknowledged the man, listened to his complaint, and then took the time to explain the situation and describe why the man's unit was best equipped to help accomplish the mission.

Marshall often said that "wars are won by the side that accomplishes the impossible" and that "[t]he army with the higher breaking point wins." Throughout his career he was able to raise his troops' "breaking point" and get them "to do the impossible" by focusing on morale. And he succeeded by doing the little things, rewarding people quickly, communicating with them, and, above all else, caring about them as individuals—people who were working toward the same goals he was.

EPILOGUE

[T]he noblest Roman of them all.
—Winston Churchill (quoting Shakespeare),
reflecting on George Marshall

American democracy is the stuff Marshall is made of . . . he is Civis Americanus.
—*Time* magazine, in naming George C. Marshall
"Man of the Year" in 1943

The truly great leader overcomes all difficulties.
—George C. Marshall

✯ ✯ ✯ ✯ ✯

"Remember this," Marshall once told a class of officer candidate graduates, "the truly great leader overcomes all difficulties, and campaigns and battles are nothing but a series of difficulties to be overcome. The lack of equipment, the lack of food, the lack of this or that are only excuses; the real leader displays his qualities in his triumphs over adversity, however great it may be."

By war's end, George Marshall epitomized his own definition of a great leader. He overcame every difficulty, persevered through every campaign and battle, and delivered only results—never excuses.

Upon his retirement from the army, President Truman said of him, "In a war unparalleled in magnitude and horror, millions of Americans gave their country outstanding service. General George C. Marshall gave it victory." His British counterparts sent him a cable that read in part: "[Y]our unfailing wisdom, high principles, and breadth of view have commanded the deepest respect and admiration of us all. Always you have honored us by your frankness, charmed us by your courtesy, and inspired us by your singleness of purpose and your devotion to our common cause."

The cable concluded with a short poem written more than two hundred years earlier by Alexander Pope. It spoke directly to many of Marshall's key leadership principles—candor, action, integrity, and selflessness:

> . . .[F]riend to truth! of soul sincere,
>> In action faithful, and in honor clear;
>>> Who broke no promise, serv'd no private end,
>>> Who gain'd no title, and who lost no friend.

Still, after receiving these glowing tributes, Marshall recognized his job was not done. He realized that it was not enough to win the war; he had to help win the peace. He therefore accepted President Truman's offer to continue to serve his country—and the world—as a statesman of peace and focused his considerable talents and energies on nurturing the conditions under which peace and prosperity could flourish.

On December 10, 1953, his work at long last complete, he traveled to Oslo, Norway to accept the Nobel Peace Prize for "the most constructive, peaceful work we have seen in this century"—the Marshall Plan.

For all of his accomplishments, Marshall's extraordinary legacy remains largely unknown to most Americans. In his *Smithsonian* article "George C. Marshall: The Last Great American?" Lance Morrow cited a quote from *Tao Te Ching* that,

I believe, captures the essence of why this is: "The master doesn't talk, he acts; when his work is done, the people say, 'Amazing: We did it all by ourselves.'"

And while Marshall would never say—nor am I suggesting—that he alone was responsible for the Allied victory in World War II, or for achieving the lasting peace that the Marshall Plan helped create, he did accomplish a great deal, and he did it quietly.

For it was George Marshall who built an enduring organization—the U.S. Army—that has helped preserve a general peace for the past six-and-a-half decades. It was George Marshall who trained a generation of leaders, including Dwight D. Eisenhower, the future president of the United States, and two future secretaries of state, Dean Acheson and Dean Rusk, who continued his work. And it was George Marshall who established a model and a framework—with the Marshall Plan and the creation of NATO—for achieving a lasting peace.

He did all of this—and so much more—by adhering to nine distinct leadership principles:

* Doing the Right Thing: The Principle of Integrity

* Mastering the Situation: The Principle of Action

* Serving the Greater Good: The Principle of Selflessness

* Speaking Your Mind: The Principle of Candor

* Laying the Groundwork: The Principle of Preparation

* Sharing Knowledge: The Principle of Learning and Teaching

* Choosing and Rewarding the Right People: The Principle of Fairness

* Focusing on the Big Picture: The Principle of Vision

* Supporting the Troops: The Principle of Caring

After Marshall retired, General Walter Bedell Smith wrote him a letter that read, in part:

> I doubt if you ever could realize the deep and sincere affection you inspired, particularly in those of us who had the good fortune to serve directly under you. I wish that I could be like you. I never can, of course, because I have a bad temper, and get irritable over small things, but I have tried very hard to be, and will continue to do so, as long as I live.

It is a wonderful passage because it still holds true. Very few people will ever "be like" George Catlett Marshall. But, like Bedell Smith, we shouldn't stop trying "very hard" to emulate him. At the beginning of this book, I quoted Ralph Waldo Emerson: "Great men exist that there may be greater men." The world will continue to need great men and women—in all walks of life—and if we adhere to George Marshall's nine leadership principles we, too, can overcome all difficulties, triumph over adversity, and make the world a better place for current and future generations.

Notes

GEORGE C. MARSHALL: THE INDISPENSABLE MAN

1. Ed Cray, *General of the Army: George C. Marshall, Soldier and Statesman* (New York: Cooper Square Press, 1990), pp. 553–554.

2. Diane B. Kunz, "The Marshall Plan Reconsidered: A Complex of Motives," *Foreign Affairs* (May/June 1997).

3. Cray, *General of the Army: George C. Marshall, Soldier and Statesman*, p. 575.

4. Forrest C. Pogue, *George C. Marshall: Statesman* (New York: Viking Press, 1987), p. xi.

CHAPTER 1

1. Mark A. Stoler, *George C. Marshall: Soldier-Statesman of the American Century* (New York: Twayne Publishers, 1989), p. 81.

2. Ed Cray, *General of the Army: George C. Marshall, Soldier and Statesman* (New York: Cooper Square Press, 1990), p. 206.

3. Edgar F. Puryear, *19 Stars: A Study in Military Character and Leadership* (New York: Ballantine Books, 1971), p. 67.

4. Cray, *General of the Army: George C. Marshall, Soldier and Statesman*, p. 148.

5. Forrest C. Pogue, *George C. Marshall: Ordeal and Hope* (New York: Viking Press, 1966), p. 93.

6. Bill George, *Authentic Leadership: Rediscovering the Secrets to Creating Lasting Value* (San Francisco: Jossey-Bass, 2003), p. 129.

7. Larry Johnson and Bob Phillips, *Absolute Honesty: Building a Corporate Culture That Values Straight Talk and Rewards Integrity* (New York: AMACOM, 2003), p. 177.

8. Cheryl Dahle, "Gap's New Look: The See-Through," *Fast Company* (September 2004), pp. 69–71.

9. Bill George, "The Journey to Authenticity," *Leader to Leader* (Winter 2004), p. 32.

10. Larry Bossidy and Ram Charan, *Execution: The Discipline of Getting Things Done* (New York: Crown Business, 2002), pp. 78–79.

11. Warren Blank, *The 108 Skills of Natural Born Leaders* (New York: AMACOM, 2001), p. 144.

12. Peter F. Drucker, "What Makes an Effective Executive," *Harvard Business Review* (June 2004), p. 60.

13. Betsy Bernard, "The Seven Golden Rules of Leadership," *FDU Magazine* (Fall/Winter 2003); a copy of her speech, as published in Fairleigh Dickinson University's magazine, is available at http://www.fdu.edu/newspubs/magazine/03fa/rules.html.

CHAPTER 2

1. Mark A. Stoler, *George C. Marshall: Soldier-Statesman of the American Century* (New York: Twayne Publishers, 1989), p. 155.

2. Lance Morrow, "George Marshall: The Last Great American?" *Smithsonian* (August 1997).

3. William A. Cohen, *The Art of the Strategist: 10 Essential Principles for Leading Your Company to Victory* (New York: AMACOM, 2004), p. 43.

4. Warren Bennis, *On Becoming a Leader* (Cambridge: Perseus Books, 1989), p. 87.

5. Alison Overholt, "The Housewife Who Got Up Off the Couch," *Fast Company* (September 2004), p. 94.

6. Edgar F. Puryear, *19 Stars: A Study in Military Character and Leadership* (New York: Ballantine Books, 1971), p. 45.

7. Bennis, *On Becoming a Leader*, p. 142.

8. Larry Johnson and Bob Phillips, *Absolute Honesty: Building a Corporate Culture That Values Straight Talk and Rewards Integrity* (New York: AMACOM, 2003), pp. 192–193.

9. Bill George, *Authentic Leadership: Rediscovering the Secrets to Creating Lasting Value* (San Francisco: Jossey-Bass, 2003), p. 135.

10. Bette Price and George Ritcheske, *True Leaders: How Exceptional CEOs and Presidents Make a Difference by Building People and Profits* (Chicago: Dearborn Press, 2001), p. 55.

11. Bennis, *On Becoming a Leader*, pp. 88–89.

12. Noel M. Tichy with Eli Cohen, *The Leadership Engine: How Winning Companies Build Leaders at Every Level* (New York: HarperCollins, 1997), pp. 130–131.

13. Ibid, p. 161.

CHAPTER 3

1. Lance Morrow, "George Marshall: The Last Great American?" *Smithsonian* (August 1997).

2. Edgar F. Puryear, *19 Stars: A Study in Military Character and Leadership* (New York: Ballantine Books, 1971), p. 70.

3. Jim Collins, *Good to Great: Why Some Companies Make the Leap . . . and Others Don't* (New York: HarperCollins, 2001), p. 28.

4. Daniel Roth, "Larry Bird Finds Trump in His Backyard," *Fortune* (May 31, 2004), p. 40.

5. Bill George, "The Journey to Authenticity," *Leader to Leader* (Winter 2004), p. 32.

6. Bette Price and George Ritcheske, *True Leaders: How Exceptional CEOs and Presidents Make a Difference by Building People and Profits* (Chicago: Dearborn Press, 2001), p. 19.

7. Cheryl Dahle, "On Thin Ice," *Fast Company* (September 2004), p. 81.

8. Puryear, *19 Stars: A Study in Military Character and Leadership*, p. 71.

9. Wendy Lubetkin, *World Leaders, Past and Present: George Marshall* (New York: Chelsea House Publishers, 1989), p. 7.

CHAPTER 4

1. Ed Cray, *General of the Army: George C. Marshall, Soldier and Statesman* (New York: Cooper Square Press, 1990), p. 152.

2. Edgar F. Puryear, *19 Stars: A Study in Military Character and Leadership* (New York: Ballantine Books, 1971), p. 83.

3. Cray, *General of the Army: George C. Marshall, Soldier and Statesman*, p. 368.

4. Ibid, p. 317.

5. Robert Mai and Alan Akerson, *The Leader as Communicator: Strategies and Tactics to Build Loyalty, Focus Effort, and Spark Creativity* (New York: AMACOM, 2003), p. 189.

6. Chuck Salter, "Mr. Inside Speaks Out," *Fast Company* (September 2004), p. 93.

7. Noel Tichy and Ram Charan, "Speed, Simplicity, Self-Confidence: An Interview with Jack Welch," *Harvard Business Review* (September/October 1989).

8. Larry Bossidy and Ram Charan, *Execution: The Discipline of Getting Things Done* (New York: Crown Business, 2002), pp. 49–50.

9. Warren Bennis, *On Becoming a Leader* (Cambridge: Perseus Books, 1989), p. 89.

CHAPTER 5

1. Edgar F. Puryear, *19 Stars: A Study in Military Character and Leadership* (New York: Ballantine Books, 1971), p. 48.

2. Mark A. Stoler, *George C. Marshall: Soldier-Statesman of the American Century* (New York: Twayne Publishers, 1989), p. 40.

3. Forrest C. Pogue, *George C. Marshall: Organizer of Victory* (New York: Viking Press, 1973), p. 14.

4. Ed Cray, *General of the Army: George C. Marshall, Soldier and Statesman* (New York: Cooper Square Press, 1990), pp. 343–344.

5. Ibid, p. 344.

6. Jon Goldberg, speaking at an American Management Association Fall 2002 Current Issues Breakfast Briefing on crisis planning; AMA events coverage available at www.amanet.org/editorial/goldberg.htm.

7. Peter Schwartz, *The Art of the Long View: Paths to Strategic Insights for Yourself and Your Company* (New York: Doubleday, 1996).

8. Noel M. Tichy with Eli Cohen, *The Leadership Engine: How Winning Companies Build Leaders at Every Level* (New York: HarperCollins, 1997), p. 120.

9. Betsy Bernard, "The Seven Golden Rules of Leadership," *FDU Magazine* (Fall/Winter 2003); a copy of her speech, as published in Fairleigh Dickinson University's magazine, is available at http://www.fdu.edu/newspubs/magazine/03fa/rules.html.

CHAPTER 6

1. Edgar F. Puryear, *19 Stars: A Study in Military Character and Leadership* (New York: Ballantine Books, 1971), pp. 49–50.

2. Forrest C. Pogue, *George C. Marshall: Education of a General* (New York: Viking Press, 1963), p. 346.

3. Pogue, *George C. Marshall: Education of a General*, p. 98.

4. Forrest C. Pogue, *George C. Marshall: Organizer of Victory* (New York: Viking Press, 1973), p. 508.

5. Puryear, *19 Stars: A Study in Military Character and Leadership*, p. 100.

6. Pogue, *George C. Marshall: Education of a General*, p. 192.

7. Wendy Lubetkin, *World Leaders, Past and Present: George Marshall* (New York: Chelsea House Publishers, 1989), p. 56.

8. Pogue, *George C. Marshall: Education of a General*, p. 192.

9. Mark A. Stoler, *George C. Marshall: Soldier-Statesman of the American Century* (New York: Twayne Publishers, 1989), p. 56.

10. Forrest C. Pogue, *George C. Marshall: Ordeal and Hope* (New York: Viking Press, 1966), p. 139.

11. Andrew Jackson Goodpaster, speech given on November 5, 1993 at the George C. Marshall Lecture in Vancouver, Washington.

12. Jim Collins, *Good to Great: Why Some Companies Make the Leap . . . and Others Don't* (New York: HarperCollins, 2001), p. 28.

13. Brent Schlender, "How the Chips Were Won," *Business 2.0* (January 2004) p. 111.

14. Noel M. Tichy with Eli Cohen, *The Leadership Engine: How Winning Companies Build Leaders at Every Level* (New York: HarperCollins, 1997), p. 102.

15. Larry Bossidy and Ram Charan, *Execution: The Discipline of Getting Things Done* (New York: Crown Business, 2002), pp. 78–79.

16. Bette Price and George Ritcheske, *True Leaders: How Exceptional CEOs and Presidents Make a Difference by Building People and Profits* (Chicago: Dearborn Press, 2001), p. 89.

17. Pogue, *George C. Marshall: Education of a General*, p. 102.

18. Warren Bennis, *On Becoming a Leader* (Cambridge, MA: Perseus Books, 1989), p. 89.

CHAPTER 7

1. Forrest C. Pogue, *George C. Marshall: Ordeal and Hope* (New York: Viking Press, 1966), p. 409.

2. Ed Cray, *General of the Army: George C. Marshall, Soldier and Statesman* (New York: Cooper Square Press, 1990), pp. 174–175.

3. Edgar F. Puryear, *19 Stars: A Study in Military Character and Leadership* (New York: Ballantine Books, 1971), p. 100.

4. Forrest C. Pogue, *George C. Marshall: Organizer of Victory* (New York: Viking Press, 1973), p. 191.

5. Pogue, *George C. Marshall: Organizer of Victory*, pp. 78–79.

6. Erick Schonfeld, "The Wizard of POS," *Business 2.0* (April 2004), pp. 100–105.

7. Chuck Salter, "Customer-Centered Leader," *Fast Company* (October 2004), p. 83.

8. Alison Overholt, "Are You a Polyolefin Optimizer? Take this Quiz," *Fast Company* (April 2004), p. 37.

9. Larry Bossidy and Ram Charan, *Execution: The Discipline of Getting Things Done* (New York: Crown Business, 2002), p. 111.

10. Noel M. Tichy with Eli Cohen, *The Leadership Engine: How Winning Companies Build Leaders at Every Level* (New York: HarperCollins, 1997), p. 149.

11. Bossidy and Charan, *Execution: The Discipline of Getting Things Done*, p. 60.

CHAPTER 8

1. Mark A. Stoler, *George C. Marshall: Soldier-Statesman of the American Century* (New York: Twayne Publishers, 1989), pp. 127–129.

2. Peter F. Drucker, "What Makes an Effective Executive?" *Harvard Business Review* (June 2004), p. 60.

3. Warren Blank, *The 108 Skills of Natural Born Leaders* (New York: AMACOM, 2001), p. 126.

4. Larry Bossidy and Ram Charan, *Execution: The Discipline of Getting Things Done* (New York: Crown Business, 2002), pp. 46–50.

CHAPTER 9

1. Forrest C. Pogue, *George C. Marshall: Ordeal and Hope* (New York: Viking Press, 1966), p. 100.

2. Edgar F. Puryear, *19 Stars: A Study in Military Character and Leadership* (New York: Ballantine Books, 1971), pp. 50–52.

3. Pogue, *George C. Marshall: Ordeal and Hope*, p. 109.

4. Ibid, p. 119.

5. William Frye, *Marshall: Citizen Soldier* (Indianapolis: Bobbs-Merrill, 1946), p. 194.

6. Forrest C. Pogue, *George C. Marshall: Education of a General* (New York: Viking Press, 1963), pp. 304–305.

7. Leonard Mosley, *Marshall: Hero for Our Times* (New York: Hearst Books, 1982), p. 343–344.

8. Ed Cray, *General of the Army: George C. Marshall, Soldier and Statesman* (New York: Cooper Square Press, 1990), p. 591.

9. Bill George, "The Journey to Authenticity," *Leader to Leader* (Winter 2004), p. 32.

10. Bette Price and George Ritcheske, *True Leaders: How Exceptional CEOs and Presidents Make a Difference by Building People and Profits* (Chicago: Dearborn Press, 2001), p. 34.

11. Price and Ritcheske, *True Leaders*, p. 141.

12. Mosley, *Marshall: Hero for Our Times*, p. 31.

13. Warren Blank, *The 108 Skills of Natural Born Leaders* (New York: AMACOM, 2001), pp. 104–105

14. Price and Ritcheske, *True Leaders*, p. 36.

15. Ibid, pp. 63–65.

16. Fiona Haley, "Mutual Benefit," *Fast Company* (October 2004), pp. 98–99.

17. Bill Breen, "The Thrill of Defeat," *Fast Company* (June 2004), pp. 77–81.

18. Larraine Segil, Marshall Goldsmith, and James Belasco, editors, *Partnering: The New Face of Leadership* (New York: AMACOM, 2003), p. 138.

19. Puryear, *19 Stars: A Study in Military Character and Leadership*, pp. 46–47.

Resources

BOOKS

Acheson, Dean. *Present at the Creation: My Years in the State Department.* New York: W. W. Norton, 1969.

Ambrose, Stephen E. *Supreme Commander: The War Years of General Dwight D. Eisenhower.* Garden City, N.Y.: Doubleday & Co., 1969.

"Biennial Report of the Chief of Staff of the United States Army to the Secretary of War, July 1, 1941 to June 30, 1943." Washington, D.C.: Government Printing Office, 1943.

Bland, Larry I. *George C. Marshall Interviews and Reminiscences for Forrest C. Pogue,* third edition, Lexington, VA: Marshall Research Foundation, 1996.

Bland, Larry I., and Sharon Ritenour Stevens, *The Papers of George Catlett Marshall,* Baltimore: Johns Hopkins University Press, 1981.

Bradley, Omar N. *A Soldier's Story.* Chicago: Rand McNally, 1951.

Cray, Ed. *General of the Army: George C. Marshall, Soldier and Statesman.* New York: Cooper Square Press, 1990.

De Weerd, H. A. *Selected Speeches and Statements of General of the Army George C. Marshall.* Washington, D.C.: Infantry Journal, 1945.

Frye, William. *Marshall: Citizen Soldier.* Indianapolis: Bobbs-Merrill, 1946.

Lubetkin, Wendy. *World Leaders, Past and Present: George Marshall.* New York: Chelsea House Publishers, 1989.

MacArthur, Douglas A. *Reminiscences.* New York: McGraw-Hill, 1964.

Marshall, Katherine T. *Together: Annals of an Army Wife.* New York: Tupper and Love, 1946.

Mosley, Leonard. *Marshall: Hero for Our Times.* New York: Hearst Books, 1982.

Payne, Robert. *The Marshall Story: A Biography of General George C. Marshall.* Englewood Cliffs, N.J.: Prentice-Hall, 1951.

Pogue, Forrest C. *George C. Marshall: Education of a General.* New York: Viking Press, 1963.

Pogue, Forrest C. *George C. Marshall: Ordeal and Hope.* New York: Viking Press, 1966.

Pogue, Forrest C. *George C. Marshall: Organizer of Victory.* New York: Viking Press, 1973.

Pogue, Forrest C. *George C. Marshall: Statesman,* 1945–1959. New York: Viking Press, 1987.

Puryear, Edgar F. *19 Stars: A Study in Military Character and Leadership.* New York: Ballantine Books, 1971.

Stoler, Mark A. *George C. Marshall: Soldier-Statesman of the American Century.* New York: Twayne Publishers, 1989.

Wilson, Rose P. *General Marshall Remembered.* Englewood Cliffs, N.J.: Prentice-Hall, 1968.

MAGAZINE ARTICLES

Chace, James. "Marshall Plan Commemorative Section: An Extraordinary Partnership: Marshall and Acheson," *Foreign Affairs* (May/June 1997).

Kindleberger, Charles P. "Marshall Plan Commemorative Section: In the Halls of the Capitol: A Memoir," *Foreign Affairs* (May/June 1997).

Kunz, Diane B. "Marshall Plan Commemorative Section: The Marshall Plan Reconsidered: A Complex of Motives." *Foreign Affairs,* May/June 1997.

Marshall, George C. "The Bitter Lesson of Unpreparedness." *Military Review* (July-August 1997), pp. 136–138.

Morrow, Lance. "George Marshall: The Last Great American?" *Smithsonian* (August 1997).

"Person of the Year, 1943: George C. Marshall." *Time* magazine (January 3, 1944); available from the *Time* archive at http://www.time.com/time/personoftheyear/archive/stories/1943.html.

"Person of the Year, 1947: George C. Marshall." *Time* magazine (January 5, 1948); available from the *Time* archive at http://www.time.com/time/personoftheyear/archive/stories/1947.html.

WEB SITES

George C. Marshall Foundation (www.marshallfoundation.org).

George C. Marshall Lecture Series, Vancouver, Washington (www.ci.vancouver.wa.us/marshall/marshall.htm).

Index

Fort Moultrie, South Carolina, 18,
   38–39, 71
Fort Reno, Oklahoma territory, 206,
   218
Fort Scriven, Georgia, 18
Fort Vancouver, Washington, 18, 39,
   212
France
   Germany and, 104–105, 107,
      127–128, 169–170
   in World War I, 17, 67, 101–102,
      124–125, 184
   in World War II, 22, 78–80,
      95–96, 169

Gap Inc., 46
Genencor International, 221–222
General Electric Company, 73, 91,
   110, 113, 133, 154, 155,
   174–175, 195–196
General Motors, 70, 71, 110
George, Bill, 44–45, 47, 111, 115, 217
Germany
   Berlin airlift crisis, 26, 65
   France and, 104–105, 107,
      127–128, 169–170
   "Germany-first" strategy, 6,
      20–21, 78, 103–105, 151–152,
      186–189, 195, 198, 200
   Great Britain and, 20–21,
      104–105, 130, 186, 188, 195
   invasion of Poland (1939), 11, 19
   postwar occupation of, 136–137
   Soviet Union and, 20, 106–107,
      113–114, 130, 186
   surrender of, 80
Gilette, 90
Gleevec, 68
Goizueta, Roberto, 69, 91
Goldberg, Jon, 131–132
Gorelick, Jamie, 50
Grant, Ulysses S., 71–72
Great Britain
   Germany and, 20–21, 104–105,
      130, 186, 188, 195
   Marshall Plan and, 63–64, 95–96
   Marshall's study of military, 122, 123
Greece, 63–64

Grove, Andy, 194
Groves, Leslie, 190–191
Grundhofer, Jerry, 155

Hagan, John C., 3
Hambly, Ann, 217–218
Harvard University, 12, 108, 116–117
Henry, Vicki, 218
Herman Miller, 93
Herring, Jim, 90
Hewlett-Packard, 222
Hitler, Adolf, 25
Home Depot, The, 154, 155
Honeywell, 134, 177, 220
Houghton, Amo, 45–46
Hurd, Mark, 175
Hutson, Nancy, 222

Iacocca, Lee, 177
Illinois National Guard, 18, 86
Immelt, Jeffrey, 133, 154
integrity, 33–53
   of Marshall, 7, 12–13, 33–44, 52–53
   other examples of, 44–51
Intel Corporation, 48, 156, 157, 194
Iraq War, 46–47, 95, 109, 137
isolationism, 19, 126
Israel, 94–95

J. Lyons & Company, 49
Japan
   atomic bomb and, 22, 43,
      190–192, 198
   Pearl Harbor, 36, 50, 151, 185, 214
   postwar occupation of, 136–137
   in Russo-Japanese War, 122–123
jeep, development of, 62–63, 66
Jenner, William, 87
JetBlue Airways, 154, 220
Johnson, Larry, 68
Johnson, Louis, 39–40
Johnson & Johnson, 67–68, 69–70
Joice, Elizabeth, 45
Jomini, Henri de, 145
Jones, Reginald, 174–175
Josaitis, Eleanor, 66–67
Joss, Bob, 155
Joyce, Kenyon, 85